Christ Rediscovered:
The Theory of Spiritual Evolution

by
Remy Theberge

PublishAmerica
Baltimore

© 2004 by Remy Theberge.
All rights reserved. No part of this book may be reproduced, stored in a retrieval system or transmitted in any form or by any means without the prior written permission of the publishers, except by a reviewer who may quote brief passages in a review to be printed in a newspaper, magazine or journal.

First printing

ISBN: 1-4137-2818-9
PUBLISHED BY PUBLISHAMERICA, LLLP
www.publishamerica.com
Baltimore

Printed in the United States of America

Dedication

DEDICATION TO A DOMINEERING TRIUMVIRATE
   Foremost, FAITH, this elusive substance that has always clung to my being as barnacles clinging to the hulk of a ship.
   Not too distant, FREEDOM OF THOUGHT, this gadfly gift deserving high accolades and which has both plagued and pleased the ever-searching horizons of my mind as life unfolded.
   Lastly and lastingly, THE MIRACLE, to be honored as the ultimate tool that granted "birth" to this book for it is that never-faded and enduring image of a young boy embracing, and being embraced, by this MIRACLE that served in launching and completing this literary venture nearly seven decades following the event.
   FAITH, FREEDOM OF THOUGHT (AND CHOICE), A PERSONAL MIRACLE, are the indispensable ingredients that produced this work and testament.

THE AUTHOR
IN THE SUMMER OF THE YEAR 2003
ATTLEBORO, MASSACHUSETTS

Laissez-Moi Pas Souffrir Le Reste De Ma Vie!

Last echo of an ancient supplication
On the shores of the St. Lawrence River
Summer of 1936

CONTENTS:

PROLOGUE..09

BOOK ONE

REFLECTIONS OF A 21ST CENTURY CATHOLIC & HERETIC.........13
IN THE BEGINNING...17
A START AND A GATHERING OF THINKERS...................................19
GROWTH, DOUBTS, AND THE BURDEN OF PROGRESS: THE FORMATIVE YEARS...25
THE CHURCH AND ITS LOVE OF MONEY...30
ABSOLUTION BY RATION..34
THE BEAUTY OF CRUELTY...37
HUMANITY'S CRAVEN ABATTOIR..40
PRIESTHOOD WITH A PURPOSE..43
GUADALUPE...47
STE. BERNADETTE SOUBIROUS (1843-1879).................................49
STE. ANNE: A PERSONAL MIRACLE..53

BOOK TWO

EARLY ECHOES FROM JERUSALEM..65
PROCEEDING TO ANTIOCH..69
FACING CHRIST AS AN EQUAL..72
CHRIST REVISITED...75
THIS SEEDLING CALLED JUDAISM...79
A TOUGH TASK: CHOOSING THE CHOSEN ONE................................81
A PARTING GLANCE AT EVOLUTION..84
STRANGE BEDFELLOWS: THE POPE AND MARTIN LUTHER.......86

CONTRADICTORY SENTIMENTS
EVERY MAN'S EPITAPH
HAIL DEATH'S SWEET EMBRACE THAT FREES MAN FROM LIFE'S BONDAGE

FAREWELL AND GREETINGS: THE CONSTANT SOLSTICE
TOO SOON CLOAKED IN THE VESTMENT OF OLD AGE, BENEATH A BRITTLE BREAST BEATS THE HEART OF A CHILD ENMESHED IN YOUTH; AND THOUGH STANDING IN THE VESTIBULE DRAPED BY MIDNIGHT, WEARY EYES STRAIN TO CONFRONT ONE MORE SUNRISE.

PROLOGUE

If a boy is raised a Catholic, as I was, in education as well as in ethnicity, then it is said quite accurately that he has been "born" a Catholic. But the verb is a grand misnomer because of my contention that a man, any man, is not born, cannot be born, in a predestined or even predictable mode. Granted, an individual is molded as his time and people and economics dictate. If I had died by age twenty or even doubled that span, it would have been direct and correct to have stated that Remy died a Catholic, and of course, a "good" Catholic at that."

But time changes in itself, and no living creature is immune to this change. His body as well as his mind, erode with the tide. But, strangely enough, the thinking process develops and undeniably peaks.

In my particular case, a major step forward evolved when I joined the military and the Air Force in my early twenties. The experience was to change me and liberate my future. I packed my bags to visit seven different air bases in three countries and two continents.

This, the simple passage of time and contact with a wider world and especially the contact with people of various backgrounds, religions, races, and ideologies, was to forever alter, for the better I know, this young man, who had formerly feared making new friends and confronting challenges and competition. For my youth, during the first two decades of life had been insulated and isolated. An existence that shunned, indeed repulsed, self-development and education. A life that actually fled before the new and unknown.

Glancing back, it is not difficult to recall the frightening prospect that awaited me and so many others of my generation and ethnic group. We were expected to obtain menial jobs, raise a family, and simply die after fulfilling our Easter Duties, which meant dying a good Catholic. Little else seemed to be of consequence.

It was not so much that we were told to be timid and obedient, especially to the clergy and the all-knowing Vatican scholars, but that it was a sacred duty rather than a choice. We were not encouraged to mix with the outside world; we did not question our superiors, especially the priests. We kept distant of sins and sinners without quite knowing where these evils lurked. We were to be wary of outsiders such as Protestants and atheists.

So we confessed our sins in the secrecy of the confessional box and emerged to sin some more, but always on the sly. We attended Mass every Sunday; all of this served in making us good Catholics and worthy of heaven after death. We qualified for burial in "holy ground." We also had to latch onto a steady job that awaited us every Monday morning; this rendered us useful citizens with just enough money rolling in to care for our daily needs and survival.

This, weekly church attendance and a steady job, seemed to constitute all that was necessary to be called a success. If we never earned a million bucks and never became famous, well that was God's will and a humility and simplicity that the angels smiled upon. Even if life on earth was harsh and dreary, even dreadful, again it was God's will and heaven would make it up to all of us AFTER death. Always it was a reward that awaited us at a future time and place.

From this simple lot and flock emerged a few priests, even a few political leaders and a few professionals. But always, it seemed, only very few compared to the large numbers involved. It was a heritage bestowed by the world into which our birth had randomly, or by choice, hurled us.

But leaving Maine and the Franco American society and its Catholic atmosphere, brought a sudden and sharp change in a thoughtful and troubled young man whose mind was now exposed to outside influences of all hues and shapes. It resulted in my Declaration of Independence, so to speak. The many thoughts that plagued my mind, finally dared to break loose from their chains. It allowed me to meet some "heavy" thinkers, who, like myself were bothered by thoughts of religious fervor as well as rebelliousness.

At this early stage I was still haunted by the idea of having rejected a priesthood to which I had been destined and obligated. But a Jewish acquaintance my own age that crossed my path shared much the identical tremors in different ways. His parents had wanted him to become a rabbi, an idea that he had resisted. I even encountered a self-proclaimed atheist, anathema to my kiln, who was surprisingly supportive to my cause—and just as knowledgeable as I considered myself to be. And behold! A likable chap. His disbelief was actually his brand of faith.

All in all, I learned that all men, all of us, are much the same no matter our origins. And as important as religion may be to some of us, it remains a secondary source, a tool, perhaps a major one at times, in a chest full of tools. The Jew and the Christian, the Muslim and the Hindu, the black and the white. We are all passengers aboard the same ship sailing over the same seas seeking the same destination.

BOOK ONE

CHAPTER ONE
REFLECTIONS OF A 21ST CENTURY CATHOLIC & HERETIC

Never would this work have been composed if my faith in God had been lacking to the slightest degree. It is, principally, a labor of love based on a lifetime's observation of life as it enshrouds and manipulates our brief journey from cradle to grave. In my particular case, Christianity and Catholicism were my main motivators and most powerful ones at that. Yet, with the passage of time and the accumulation of knowledge, surprisingly and without design, other faiths and "gods" were to encroach upon the mental landscape. There existed other winds and storms, beyond the Catholic firmament, to pummel thoughts and uproot a previously set mind frame.

I came to understand that I was but one man walking one path leading to the identical mutual destination, desired by others just as devout and believing as I was, even others who had never heard of Christ or even detested my religion for whatever reason. Prejudice and injustice prevailed everywhere, but so did good and fairness. Evil and its clinging companion, sin, were equally overpowering forces that permeated our existence.

There was this everlasting struggle between the good angels and bad angels, whose cries of lamentations and supplications echoed from the most ancient biblical text. It was difficult to separate our lives from fairy tales simply because our lives were a fairy tale. How else can be explained the beauty of a Cinderella? Seen in a young, pretty, vivacious girl, and again, the very real threat and evil of an unseen "demon" that all of us somehow truly feel and sense in our everyday existence. Superstition gives way to fascination. Our lives are strangely beyond our physical grasp. We see not what our eyes see, but what lies beyond our range of vision.

Life, I came to understand was a tribulation, but one obviously worthy of a devoted struggle in order to overcome humanity's shortcomings and to triumph in the end. How else could it be? What else could matter?

So I cast a backward glance at my Catholic past in order to uncover both motive and purpose to my existence. And I found myself, surprisingly at first, criticizing the time-honored ways of my forefathers' beloved religion that had been my own inheritance. Despite the fact that ceremonies are very important, I came to picture sacraments, especially confession and the

Eucharist, as more symbolic than realistic. I could not accept the Last Rite as the ultimate tool that could either save or doom me for eternity.

My heresy was secret and personal. And, until I penetrated well into my forties, a very disturbing and clandestine experience. But it was also an awakening and a revealing rebellion that evolved into an established way of life. It was not my religion that I was questioning and criticizing. It was not priests or bishops or popes that I was belittling. It was not the tenets of my faith that I was denigrating. It was simply that I wanted to be myself without the imposition of interference from an outside force that was an organized religion with all its laws and regulations, designed to delegate the faithful flock into a shaky slot of pending sin and guilt. In turn, which placed the priest on a pedestal of righteousness and the penitent in a straitjacket of obedience. It was a game of mind-control played on a grand scale. And all the other major religious groups played the same tune.

Rome and the Vatican claimed a sort of majestic manifest destiny orchestrated to religious structures. The pope claimed the Divine Rights of Kings reserved to the chief apostle, Peter, who was commissioned by Jesus Himself to preach the word and save the world from Satan and his henchmen. There was little room for individualism. It was all lofty and impressive—as well as incomplete. In my layman's mind, developing and questing, Peter could have died as some of his fellow apostles, a more devout Jew than a firebrand Christian preacher, despite his reported martyr in Rome and his own head-downward crucifixion.

That Simon Peter was special. There seems to be little doubt that Jesus ordered him to "feed my sheep" is a most credible assumption. But always, a man two millennia later is left to guess the exact meaning to man and message, just as he is left dangling as to Christ's exact origin and being.

Suffice to say that history has recorded the existence of two beings that were instrumental in changing our world for the better. Even though some ardent Christian historians, such as Albert Schweitzer, claimed that a historical Jesus cannot be proven. I accept His reality and His life.

Always, it is a matter of faith and how this faith molds our existence. No two men "see" God in the same light. No two men feel or sense religion in a similar fashion. Yet it can be argued that a Muslim's inner vision of Allah mirrors that of a Christian saint's concept of an inner Christ. It all boils down to independent choice and "gut" feeling for this inner vision and no priest can infringe upon this birthright.

I've been a Sunday lector at my home parish of St. Stephen in Attleboro for over a decade now. I volunteered for the chore following a public appeal for speakers of the word. Now, upon publication of this work that will reveal my indifference for the sacraments, and my absence from the confessional box for a quarter of a century; at this writing I will be obliged to resign my lectureship. For whoever heard of a Catholic lector who hasn't attended confession for twenty-five years?

Not to mention the "sacrilegious" communion hosts that I periodically receive both for show and reverence in the memory of my father and more ancient ancestors who loved and believed in the sacrament.

I'll be called a liar, a hypocrite, and of course, an unfeeling, unrepentant heretic. But I neither see nor accept the accusations as proffered. Quite simply, I am a traditional Catholic and always will be happy to be called a Catholic. I enjoy my assignments as speaker quoting biblical passages. I believe in the "word." A man must attempt to inject his small contributions.

I don't deny that perhaps I should, at the offset, have informed the pastor of my particular background and feelings that would have certainly disqualified me for the task at hand. But I felt, and still feel, that sincere action is more important than passive inaction. As long as the subject was not raised, as long as I was not directly asked, I did not feel an obligation to "confess" my religious pedigree and unique personal religiosity.

It will hurt me to be forcibly retired from my role as lector, for I both enjoy and believe in the work. But I do predict with certainty that less than a century following my death an unceremonious and unsacramental Catholic as myself, today, will be both welcome and respected by the institutional church. Indeed, I believe that most Catholics of that not-so-distant day will constitute the vast majority of the faithful that enter and kneel in the solace of a chapel, in order to share a few moments with an unseen power.

I saw it all happen before as a young boy who was taught by the Dominican nuns to shun the Protestant Church down the road from our school (and which I promptly visited). This was an age long predating the Ecumenical Council, convened by Pope John 23rd in 1962 that saw the rapprochement of the various faiths. At long last, a rabbi and priest, or Protestant minister, could enter a synagogue or Baptist church to pray, marry, even baptize. A later pope, John Paul II, would preach in a Lutheran church in Rome.

All this I saw occur during my lifetime. This, and much more. For life and faith feed upon the same fruit and seek the same fate. One cannot thrive without the other. Faith laces life with this essential element that may be called the bale of humanity. This unsacramental, but hardly irreligious and irreverent lector preaching before the throng in a small church has felt both its power and its call to duty.

In the end, a man proceeds as both heart and soul dictate. It is a matter of life betrothed to faith and its forceful plunge into the abyss that awaits all of us. But, to the believer, it is an abyss spilling over into a lasting land of warmth and sunshine.

This inheritance is mankind's prized endowment and the zenith of creation. Rather than our mutual expedition into oblivion, life constitutes our mutual caravan beyond the cosmos. It is our love-affair with the unending, our hope and promise of affinity tied to eternity, our flirtation with the great unseen.

CHAPTER TWO
IN THE BEGINNING...

Every man seeks to instill some momentum into his existence, to this reason that justifies his being alive. In essence, meaning to his life. And the search seems unending. For it is a search for one's own brand of truth, and this truth is evasive. It is a friend that seeks solitude before yielding to intimacy.

This work is an attempt to unravel this mystery that dwells within every individual. It is a search for light before darkness engulfs. It is a journey of discovery before I winter into the depths of my disappearance.

My being raised and educated a Catholic of the old school wedged me into a tight harness where liberating thoughts were not only discouraged but condemned. The road map of your life had been prepared by learned and saintly men (always men, it seemed, even with the Blessed Virgin's importance in my religious culture). You were expected to follow a straight pathway. Lest you be branded a hardhead or worse.

But, from my earliest age, I was a questioner with an inquisitive mind of what, I was to later learn, was considered erratic and heretic. If you dared rock the boat, you had to be prepared to be cast overboard.

I was the type who had to dispense with my fears and despair in order to pursue my own identity. My church was imposing its own brand of spiritual manifest destiny as applied to the physical. But the weight of my mental energy, in the form of inexhaustible queries, was more than a match for the formidable task confronting me. I had to overcome a long-established and entrenched authority in order to unearth my own.

I had to be my own man even while still a boy, at the expense, I was fully aware, of being considered an outcast by my peers.

A prime credo of my upbringing was that submissiveness (to church) was perfection (to God). But I found this prospect both unappealing and unnecessary. The very idea made me sulk. I decided that I could be both a devout Catholic (in my own fashion) and a questioning heretic, without betraying my heritage.

So here I stood in the 1930s, unassuming and stubborn, a Franco American lad who dared go his own way and be himself. For the time and place, a tall order even when pursued in secrecy. And my staunch independence would never waver.

At this point, I feel it is of utter necessity to exhibit a bit of personal background and some sources of information that have influenced this writer and budding philosopher in tackling his work. It is a definite case of establishing authenticity while avoiding braggadocio. The reader MUST know, or feel, that the scribbling chronicler and thinker is sincere. That he is in something more than disagreement for its own sake and pleasure. Indeed, what great thinkers and philosophers have served in molding my life and thoughts?

I would venture to say that literally thousands of individuals and their thoughts have passed my eyes. I would be at a loss to name but a small percentage of these acquaintances. The enumeration would fill pages with an aura of boredom rather than grandeur. It would be a form of boasting for its own purpose, which is hardly the case.

Still, the reader deserves a certain measure of confidence afforded by the knowledge that the author is knowledgeable and sincere, educated, and serious in his endeavor.

Following is a partial listing of the men whose thoughts, achievements, fame and perhaps, just an inkling of their greatness, has remained with me throughout the years. They were and remain my distant mentors, whose impact has been formidable even if it defies specific analysis.

Quite surprising to me was the emergence of the Dominican friars of my youth, these architects of the sorrowful Spanish Inquisition, who are prominent in the display.

It was stunning, really a shocking revelation, as I progressed, to realize that all, but all of my great philosophers and thinkers that influenced me were men to the core. Not a female of the species is included in my esteemed collection of lofty accomplishers that could easily number in the thousands. I suppose, accordingly, that I am predisposed to the ancient myth and dictate that it is a "man's world" and that women are subservient and somehow inferior, intellectually, to men.

The Catholic Church celebrates the celibacy of its priests. The Muslim mullahs are men, as are Tibetan monks and until recently, Jewish rabbis. All of the great Eastern religions claim their all-male teachers. In our world of philosophy and religion, it is indeed a "man's world."

CHAPTER THREE
A START AND A GATHERING OF THINKERS

Recalling personages that have influenced and energized both my mind and curiosity, and continuous questioning quest, proves a tricky tackle. Here, anyone for the sole purpose of impressing the reader, can peruse an encyclopedia of WHO'S WHO and dig out a list of important figures that have dotted the ages. I certainly referred to the expected encyclopedias in order to refresh my memory and organize my data. No name has been extracted from the list if I believed it had not crossed my eyes and study even briefly, in some cases a half-century and more ago.

Mostly, the names are vague. The applicable accomplishments just as vague. In many cases I was simply intrigued by the singsong rhythm of the listed individual. If he was French or German, he gained my immediate attention and probably my deeper scrutiny. But, always, I was "aware" of an enduring contribution. Forerunners were mathematicians, theologians and explorers. They changed so forcibly and lastingly the history of our hemisphere, especially of the Americas and Africa, almost always in the name of a Catholic monarch and Christ the Lord.

Love and tolerance were rare attributes that Magellan and Columbus appeared to treat with indifference. Cortes and Pizarro destroyed empires without apparent qualms or the fear of retribution in the hereafter. After all, Catholicism was believed to be the one true faith. The culture of the white Europeans was accepted, without question, as being superior to any other.

Those afflicted with brown or black skin were considered heathens, inferior, subhuman, dispensable trash to be cast aside or enslaved like beasts of burden.

Biologists. Physicians. Scientists. They were all present. But philosophy and philosophers were the main fare topping a meandering menu. They were my favorite heroes, especially those like Savanarola and Luther, who raised the loudest ruckus against the encroached establishment of their days at the possible cost of life and limb. Each of the names crossed my path at one time or another in some meaningful, if brief, fashion.

They were the result of my voracious reading and search for minds that had scanned my identical horizon in the hope of attaining some insight and meaning to the random existence that is thrust upon us all. The cubicle of my mind was filled with their presence as I groped to find answers, or encouragement, or inspiration, or, behold! Wisdom.

GEORGE MENDEL—19TH CENTURY CATHOLIC AUSTRIAN MONK

Credited as being the discoverer of the basis laws of heredity. There are some indications that his religious superiors disapproved of his "unauthorized" research and findings. An obedient and devout prelate, he readily accepted assignments that precluded his spending much time with his beloved experiments, especially with peas.

ST. THOMAS AQUINAS (1225-1274)

Italian philosopher known as the Angelic Doctor. A Dominican priest and professor of theology. Called "dumb ox" because he was slow and heavy, considered the most brilliant of scholastic philosophers. Famous for quote: "Evil is only the absence of good."

JOHANN GUTENBERG (c.1397-1468)

Generally accepted as inventor of the printing press in 1453 which brought books and literacy to the masses. This invention was the very first "explosion of information." Not until the advent of worldwide television and computers in the twentieth century would anything occur to surpass this achievement.

MARTIN LUTHER (1483-1546)

Great German leader of the Protestant Reformation. An Augustinian friar, in 1517 he protested the dispensation of indulgences being granted, for a monetary fee, by fellow-priest Johann Tetzel. Luther detested the papacy of his time, seeing it as a corrupt institution unworthy of the Christian mission. He seemed to have discarded the seven Catholic sacraments save baptism and marriage and preached grace of soul and redemption by Christ through the power of faith alone.

Special note: Luther emerges as an unexpected mainstay and leading character of this literary work. A later chapter deals with an in-depth analysis of his contributions and importance.

VOLTAIRE (1694-1778)

French philosopher and author. His hatred of religious and political persecution and injustice was legendary. His writing and thinking is said to have heavily influenced the French Revolution and eighteenth century Enlightenment.

WILLIAM SHAKESPEARE (1564-1616)
Greatest English poet and dramatist. Author of Macbeth, Anthony and Cleopatra, King Lear, etc. A literary genius that transcends the time.

SIGMUND FREUD (1856-1939)
The creator of modern psychoanalysis.

ALBERT EINSTEIN (d. 1955)
Famous for his theory of relativity on electrodynamics of moving bodies.

CHARLES DARWIN (d. 1882)
His theory of evolution and his famous book *The Survival of the Fittest* hardly made him a favorite of the Vatican. Darwin theorized that man evolved in the form of all animal life, high and low, which contradicted harshly with the "divine" source of creation claimed by theologians.

GIROLAMO SAVONAROLA (1452-1498)
An Italian religious reformer and another Dominican priest. During the Middle Ages he was appalled at the irreligiosity emanating from Rome. He possessed a burning eloquence and his direct attacks on moral laxity made him a popular teacher. He was particularly horrified at the immorality of Pope Alexander II and was not shy in spreading his dissatisfaction to the laymen of the land.

In the end, as might have been predicted, and doubtless with church higher-ups aiding the cause, the "rebel" teacher was tortured and hanged by the city officials of Florence.

What particularly interested me about Savonarola in my early teens, when I accidentally uncovered his name and doings, was the fact that the Christian Brothers who taught us apparently knew little or nothing about him. I belonged to a parish administered by the Dominican Order. Heretics were simply discarded, their memories buried along with their stained bones and soiled souls.

GIORDINO BRUNO (1548-1600)
An Italian philosopher, and, again, a Dominican priest. Another outspoken critic of the church who caught my eye at random. Accused of heresy, he left the order to become a wandering preacher. In his metaphysical words, he was to challenge all dogmatic authority.

Bruno proclaimed that absolute truth was beyond statement and that possible knowledge was unlimited. Seeking his own brand of truth, the church was uncomfortable with him.

Tried in Venice, he was burned at the stake, a martyr to freedom of thought. His influence on later philosophy, especially that of Spinoza and Leibnitz, was profound.

JOAN OF ARC (1412?-1431)

A French saint and national heroine, the Maid of Orleans who led the French army against the hated English. The young girl who heard and was instructed by the voices of three saints, Michael, Catherine, and Margaret— a life and deeds far stranger than fiction.

Had not every word of her irregular ecclesiastic trial at Rouen been preserved to this day, no author would dare fabricate such a harebrained plot that sees a teenage peasant girl leave her village of Domremy in Lorraine, to head military forces to victory on the field of battle. Not to mention "hearing" voices from the air.

To me, the story of Joan is studded with religious overtones. I have always been fascinated by her trial headed by bishop Pierre Cauchon who wore the defendant down over a period of several months. Found guilty of heresy and sorcery, Joan was burned at the stake.

The Vatican was forever stuck and embarrassed with its bishop cast as chief villain and prosecutor in the delicate episode. The whole event was too famous to be concealed or disguised and Cauchon's role could never be denied. For all of the voluminous information at its disposal, Rome was to wait nearly 500 years, half a millennium, to canonize Joan a saint. I am convinced that she would have attained sainthood in but a few decades had Cauchon been lacking.

NICHOLAS COPERNICAN (1473-1543)

Polish astronomer and a monk. Modern astronomy is based on his Copernician System which describes the Sun as center of a great celestial system with the Earth and other planets revolving around it. He possessed a great insight of the colliery in heavens.

SIR ISAAC NEWTON (1642-1727)

English physician, mathematician, philosopher. A great researcher and discoverer in light and calculus. Famous for the apple tumbling off his head as he rested beneath a tree in an orchard, thus precipitating the discovery of gravity.

GALILEO (1564-1642)

An Italian, whose daughter was a Dominican nun. An astronomer, mathematician, physicist. Forced by the Inquisition to abjure his belief that the Earth moved around the Sun, he was placed under house arrest for the rest of his life. His studies foreshadowed Newton's laws of motion.

FRANCISCO PIZARRO (c. 1476-1541) & HERNANDO CORTES (1485-1547)

Spanish Conquistadors. Pizarro conquered Peru and destroyed the Inca empire. Cortes overwhelmed Mexico and eradicated the Aztec presence.

Together, these two conquerors assassinated native leaders and razed their kingdoms. It is estimated by some historians that following the ravages of massive white men's diseases and warfare that better than 95 per cent of the native population perished. Of some 26 million inhabitants, fewer than a million survived the Spanish penetration.

The above entries conclude what is the author's attempt to convince the reader that he is erudite, sincere, educated, and therefore well prepared in the pursuit of his endeavor. Hopefully this goal has been achieved.

MAIN CLOSING OBSERVATIONS

It took the Catholic Church five full centuries to pronounce Joan of Arc a saint, thanks to Bishop Cauchon's lamentable role in the drama. And it took Rome four centuries to vindicate Galileo.

It was not until 1992 that Pope John Paul II formally proclaimed that the Roman Catholic Church had erred in condemning the astronomer. Speaking before the Pontifical Academy of Sciences, the pope's words were carefully selected to preserve and protect Catholic dignity: "The result," the pope stated "of tragic mutual incomprehension . . . supposed rejection of scientific progress."

The theologians of the time, he further stated, in maintaining the "centrality of the Earth," erred in thinking that the literal sense of Scriptures explained the physical world. In fact, the pontiff continued, there are two realms of knowledge, "one which has its own Revelation and one which reason can discover by its own power." The two realms are distinct but compatible, he further added.

In this light, I daresay that writing this book, which is selectively critical of certain segments of Catholic history, will be a permitted endeavor even though it will attract the scorn of many conservative Catholic theologians and scholars.

As a man piles up the years, he accepts or rejects ideals as well as principles. What was important to the lad of seven or eight often fades into obscurity. Baseball heroes as well as admired priests are but a speck in the boy-who-has-become-a-man's memory bank. And the grown-up and perhaps over mature adult gazing at the twilight of his years has suddenly developed new interests and principles that the mind, more than the body, craves and creates.

A young boy dreams of the future and seeks one filled with hope and happiness. The old man peers beyond his brittle physical existence and its last gasp, and somehow perceives an inexplicable continuation beyond a petrified body and frigid gravesite.

CHAPTER FOUR
GROWTH, DOUBTS, AND THE BURDEN OF PROGRESS: THE FORMATIVE YEARS

I do believe that embracing the distant and unchallenging, unrewarding credo of an agnostic, could have been my lot to a minimal degree, had it not been for the "miracle" that clutched my stomach so long ago on the faraway shores of the St. Lawrence River in Québec Province; on the site lying halfway between Québec City and the small village of St. Eugene where my father was born in 1898.

This "miracle" is the sole motivation propelling my pen and mind to attempt to explain and dissolve the turbulence that has plagued my thoughts throughout my lifetime. To the fore comes my unyielding independence of mind that has always asked, why? Rather than submit to blind dictates, or unquestioned authority, from whatever source.

Very early in life, during my very first years of schooling under the tutorship of strong and devout Dominican nuns hailing from the Old Country, which means France itself, I could feel my silent yet persistent, "why?" which did not conform to established Catholic method.

Even at five-years of age I could detect the rebelliousness within my "soul." I could likewise sense a deeply rooted love for this supreme being called God—He was there. He would always be there. Call Him by any other name, Christ, Allah, Yahwe, Manitou, or simply Lord or Master, but He was there.

Faith is a gift that I consider my greatest birthright and most illustrious and luminous companion. Without this faith I would classify my life as empty, sterile, and aimless. A project and journey without destination or purpose. An existence without design.

I was born at the beginning of 1929 in Brunswick, Maine, a French Canadian enclave surrounded by other such enclaves. At that period in time in that section of New England, it meant living in what had to be the center of French Catholic America. A distinction I'm sure was shared by our Cajun cousins in faraway Louisiana.

Priests. Nuns. Affiliation to parish life and education. A clannish existence permeated by a stark, rock-ribbed Catholicism that had been uprooted from France to be re-implanted in Quebec. The French language dominated in the home, the school, the playground, the workplace. You attended Mass every Sunday under the penalty of mortal sin should you stray from this sacred duty. By abiding by the rules, you were regarded as a "good Catholic." When you died you were granted a funeral Mass sung by a priest, buried in hallowed ground and assumed to have gone to heaven. The Catholic faith, you were taught and assured, guaranteed this unerring pilgrimage to Valhalla.

As a follower, you did not question the pronouncements of the church fathers; after all, the priests and bishops were the direct descendants of Christ's disciples who came to us in an unbroken chain. They could not err if only because God could not err. Or so went our indoctrination at school at the hands of the nuns—with the silent exception of this young boy and his persistent, "why?"

So here I sat in a classroom, not yet six years of age and already I had "figured out" that a God had created me and anyone else, with this freedom to choose my action and destiny. This freedom of choice was an important "understood" factor even at this early stage, just a few steps removed from babyhood.

One day, I mustered the courage to ask a devout nun-teacher, with all the boyhood piety I could manage: "Sister, what's heaven like?" Instantly, with clasped hands and eyes rolling heavenwards, the breathless nun replied, with matching piety: "Oh, my child. It's so wonderful! For all eternity you'll be adoring God!"

It was my first unsatisfactory answer to an important question and quest. Adoring God for eternity? It didn't sound too exciting; a prolonged adoring sequence leaving you with eternally sore knees; a boring, unending reward if ever one was granted. There had to be more to heaven, to life, to afterlife, to the soul itself, than the simple act of adoration. My first open query had left me in a lurch.

Now, understand, I was attempting to believe everything that was being hurled my way. It was simply that my insistence of going deeper into the subject was forever obstructing complete and final acceptance of what was being attempted to be engraved upon my youthful mind. I had already confronted this thing called freedom of choice.

I glance back over the many decades and I am actually amazed that my stubbornness and rebelliousness of will exposed itself so early in my mental and physical developing stages. I was reluctant to abandon tradition, but the process of schism had already begun.

My love for the church would endure a lifetime. My respect for the truly devoted religious would never waver. My need for authority would never diminish. Yet here I stood prepared and unfearing in not only questioning a sacrament, but actually willing to set it completely aside!

God, I accepted, would one day receive and judge me, as He will. However I unfearingly rejected, from the very start that a man and a priest and a ceremony and the simple wave of a hand, like a magical wand, could serve on my deathbed. On one hand gaining entrance into heaven or the other, condemning me to hell. It was all too simple, not to say unfair and unjust. It was all too unrealistic and preposterous. It inflamed my young mind, destined to ask so many questions as the years and life ran their course. Most disturbing to me was this element of injustice that seemed attached to the whole scheme.

My fierce doubt and dislike for the ceremony has endured throughout my life. I was never to retreat for a single day from my refusal to accept a man's wave of his hand, a priest's absolution as the determining requirement in gaining heaven or meriting hell. If the priest arrived at the bedside five minutes before death, the nun had explained, and had a chance to hear confession, where the repugnant mortal sin was admitted and absolution was granted, the dying person expired and entered heaven forthwith. But, alas! Should the priest be delayed or death hastened by five minutes, the dying person was committed to the inexhaustible fires of hell for eternity.

No! I remember whispering inwardly. No! I could not accept that a priest's presence, be he a good and saintly man at that, could dictate that heaven or hell was merited and that confession and five minutes' time, one way or the other, could likewise decide the eternal state of any human being. There had to be more to life and death than this mere ceremony that could, according to my teacher-nun, spell everlasting doom or reward.

I was never to forget that eventful day that my life entered into conflict against church doctrine, and, consequently, authority. No other day would occur abruptly, thoroughly, and enduringly. It was my first lesson to leave its lasting imprint. My revocation of the Last Rite (as a cure-all) bordered on resentment.

Papal Infallibility

That the pope can't make a mistake, in my estimation, is a mistake in fact and intent. A background study is naturally required in order to decipher this amazing dogma of dogmas.

The pronouncement is a contradiction in itself, namely, that a man can't make an error for the simple reason that he can't afford to be considered subject to the normal erratic ways of mankind. Or that, in the process of declaring himself the successor of St. Peter, and therefore the earthly replacement of Christ Himself (Christ being the flawless God or Son of God), the pope can't err because God can't err. The dogma is, to me, an unnecessary tool designed to protect the pope's "godliness."

The times that saw papal infallibility become a dogma were especially trying ones for the Church of Rome. The church fathers in the Vatican felt they were losing their iron grip on an obedient Catholic populace, which, till then, had been reasonably under control for many centuries throughout the faithbasket that comprised central and southern Europe. Now, troubling signposts emerged to drive fear into the bishops' hearts; even Luther and his Reformation had not presented a greater threat to church authority.

The faithful flock had become largely indifferent. A law that mandated strict obedience had to be created.

The ever-pressing and complex problem of harnessing tens of millions of followers had become more and more apparent to church leaders who oversaw its worldwide rule that was being more and more daringly challenged by the masses. Even Catholics dwelling in the bedrocks of Catholicism, such as existed in France and Italy, were no longer intimidated by fears of excommunication and damnation.

Sunday church attendance had gradually declined. Men, especially, were apt to be indifferent to religious practice although they were more than willing to submit to a last confession and the Last Rite on their deathbeds. Not lost, too, was the dire effect on the collection basket. A man who did not attend Mass for some decades, even if his contributions were meager, left a church with a weakened financial base.

Thus the advent of the 1870s brought a chilling realization to light as Rome assembled its cardinals and bishops to discuss the church's slip from power. Too many Catholics were willing to go their own way without fear of retribution; the coffers were only half-filled. Even revered country priests in small farming villages in an Ireland untouched by the Reformation could not expect their flocks to blindly follow exhortations.

Something drastic had to be done—and quickly—less the tragedy of Scandinavia be duplicated. The only Catholics in Sweden, for instance, were found buried in cemeteries deep beneath their Protestant descendants. A once-Catholic Iceland was now all-Protestant, its last Catholic bishop reported to have fathered some 19 children. A hated and detested cleric, he had been beheaded, along with two of his sons, by an angry mob. His death spelling the end of Iceland's Catholic heritage.

If Catholicism had been forever lost to Scandinavia, such a fate could not be allowed to occur in Catholic Europe. It was under these gloomy auspices that papal infallibility was instituted.

It was accomplished at the First Vatican Council of 1870, under the watchful eye of the iron-fisted, arch-conservative Pius IX. And despite the secrecy involved and records that have been "lost" to this day, it has been determined by some church historians that as many as two-thirds of the bishops involved in the voting resisted and opposed the dogma. In the end, intrigue, arm-twisting, and other political techniques employed by the tyrannical Pius IX served in carrying the day and establish the new rule and safeguard.

It's most interesting, to me, to note that my father, an old-school Catholic who questioned few dictates of the church, would have voted with the opposing side had he had a voice in the matter, for he once confessed to me, almost in disgust, that he found the dogma more than a bit strange.

"The pope," he stated firmly, "is a man like me, and I make mistakes!"

CHAPTER FIVE
THE CHURCH AND ITS LOVE OF MONEY

It is regrettably impossible for me to talk at length of my church without bringing money into focus. Sad, because it's a bitter bit of criticism, on my part, that I wish I could overlook and discard without elaboration. But this remains a serious work dealing with what is good, and not so good, about an ancient institution that governed much of my early childhood and that I was taught was not only sacrosanct but beyond reproach.

From my earliest boyhood, money seemed to have been of vital concern for my church; as well as the application of power and the control of the masses. Money is a most difficult and delicate subject to broach, for a dedicated parish priest must also live with the system imposed upon him. He, too, is a workingman whose wages come by way of the collection basket. He needs money to repair his church and rector, for his food and transportation, ad infinitum. All of this is understood. But the separation of need and greed soon becomes apparent as a knowledgeable Catholic layman studies the overall picture and situation, as I am doing now.

The Dominican priests of my home parish of SS. Peter & Paul, in Maine, to which I belonged for nearly 20 years, were keenly aware of the power of the dollar bill. They seldom let their flock forget it. Sunday "penny-throwers" into the basket were often openly chastised from the pulpit in abrasive fashion.

The church edifice itself was huge, really a cathedral, serving a large congregation consisting mainly of low-paid textile millworkers and shoe shop laborers. The yearly financial report to the parishioners was unfailingly predictable. The parish seemed to always break even, never a dollar left over. Although some 16,000 churchgoers consisted of the church population in its heyday, I always felt that the break-even yearly announcement, rendered with an undisguised scornful tone at the penny-throwers, while unabashedly thanking "those" who really donated, was just a bit unbelievable to my ears.

In my fiscal calculation, based on a steady weekly attendance at numerous Masses and an estimated minimum contribution by the sizable throngs, I could guess nothing but a hefty profit at year's end despite the Dominicans' wailing to the contrary.

Additionally, the parish owned a large hockey arena, St. Dominic's. This structure was busy with sports activities year-round, the building filled with well-paying sports fans reaping in a profit. And the arena had been built by labor, material, and money furnished by local benefactors. I simply found the yearly break-even reports a bit incredulous.

I never objected to my parish priest living well and comfortably, even high off the hog. I want, and expect, my bishop, as well as the pope, to be free of monetary encumbrances. The Vatican, after all has served all mankind in preserving some of the greatest achievements produced by the hands and minds of men. Sacred scrolls, ancient writings and records, artifacts, paintings and sculptures from the hands of geniuses and giants such as Rafael, Michelangelo, Titian, Leonardo da Vinci, and countless others, are but a few items to be mentioned. These are priceless treasures that MUST be saved and preserved. But, again, the argument returns to my main topic which is the abuse of money.

The ancient biblical admonition, that the love of money is the root of all evil, churns its weird echo when applied to priests and bishops as chief malefactors.

Integrated into Vatican daily operations is a huge, complex section dedicated to stock market transactions correlated with all the major financial centers of the world. State of the art computers link Tokyo, New York, London, Paris, etc. This vast monetary hookup and dealings appear to contradict Pope John Paul II's periodic warnings that neither Communism nor capitalism is an acceptable concept that can serve the ultimate betterment of mankind.

Yet one of the church's main concerns remains the might of money and its accumulation. Full-time priest-financiers operate the vast Vatican stock market network, and in recent years, a major scandal occurred when well over a billion, that's billion, dollars were discovered to be missing from the Vatican coffers.

The Italian police wanted to question a certain Lithuanian-American bishop who was suspected to have first-hand knowledge in the matter. But the Vatican quickly imposed its diplomatic immunity status and kept the bishop under wraps for some two years or longer, never allowing him to leave the safety zone until the police finally lifted their warrant for his arrest and questioning.

Such evasive tactics leave the average layman puzzled and numb—even angry. Was there something to hide? Why did the Vatican refuse to allow the authorities to question the bishop? Where's all the loot? It all leaves even a faithful Catholic with his doubts and a sour taste in his mouth. It all boils down to the matter of greed and the enormous power created but enormous funds. It is not, in my mind, the proper place for the church to be involved in major stock dealings and the unsavory surfeit of money entailed in the process.

When well over a billion dollars turns up short, and a police investigation is impeded, something is definitely awry.

Closer to home, in my city of residence in Attleboro, Mass., another case of a major money crisis involving a Catholic order surfaced a few years ago centering around the well-known and respected order of the La Salette priests.

It became a matter of public record that the order had lost some 25 million dollars in stock transactions in what appeared to be under dubious conditions. The authorities finally decided not to prosecute after a long period of deliberation. No fraud, it was declared, had been intended by the La Salette society which agreed to sell some prime properties it owned in order to alleviate matters and repay some of the bad debts incurred.

Again, we are confronted with a prime example of the church dealing in major monetary enterprises. A billion-plus. Twenty-five million. Sums that stagger the imagination of the average churchgoer and workingman who is the backbone of support for the entire organization, both spiritually and financially, and who is left out in the cold insofar explanation and justification is concerned.

It seems inappropriate for the church to be involved in monetary dealings of such magnitude. As the enraged young Jesus threw the money-changers out of the temple so long ago, I feel He could walk alongside the computer banks of the Vatican stock market section today, smashing the consoles to bits.

The love that priests reserve for money is brought to mind, but another to the Dominican friars of my old parish in Lewiston, these owners of a million-dollar sports arena named St. Dominic's.

Boxing is my favorite sport, which every so often is condemned from the pulpits of Catholic churches; the Vatican does raise its voice against the sport and the primitive brutality involving two men physically attacking each other. So, what happened? In 1965 Sonny Liston had lost his heavyweight title to the brash and cocky Muhammad Ali AKA Cassius Clay, a charismatic athlete and spokesman for black Americans.

He was also a staunch dissenter and an outspoken critic of the unpopular Vietnam war and had announced his refusal to be drafted into military service even if it spelled imprisonment. In addition to this, precipitating the adoption of his new Islamic name, Ali had just announced his membership and allegiance to the Black Muslim Party, a group that many considered not only anti-Christian but anti-American.

Politicians were up in arms and Ali was assailed from all sides. He would eventually be forced into a three-and-a-half year retirement in the very prime of his career. In the end, his popularity not only intact but enhanced, he would reappear in triumph in boxing. The politicians would be defeated by his skill and charisma.

In 1965, however, Ali was at his lowest peak of acceptance. A return bout had been signed but politics and the Black Muslim label were intervening with a site to be chosen. The cries of un-Americanism were raised all over the place. Big city after big city turned down the Ali-Liston rematch despite its great monetary appeal. The government was vigorously blacklisting the new champion from Kentucky and boxing officials were fearful of reprisals.

It was at this delicate moment that the Dominican friars of Lewiston were approached by some daring promoters. Would the priestly owners be interested in renting their St. Dominic hockey arena for a single night for a princely sum? Not to mention that the world would be watching the event.

Well, the Vatican bosses disapproved of boxing, of two men facing each other with the intent of inflicting physical harm. The church condemned such primitive encounters. The Lewiston Dominicans were doubtless aware of this official edit. But one-night's fat rental fee was anything but a throw from a penny-pitcher at the Sunday collection basket.

The point, clearly, is money and the fact that the fight was held under the auspices of the Dominican Order. Money talked louder than words or principle and the Vatican pronouncement against boxing was forgotten and ignored.

CHAPTER SIX
ABSOLUTION BY RATION

It's strange to confront the mystery of martyrdom alongside the mystery of sin, and to see, strangely enough, how one can contradict as well as compliment each other. In this instance, I face the moving episode of the young Italian girl, Maria Goretti, who was murdered in the summer of 1902 while preserving her virginity.

To me, I see an instance of a sin not quite forgiven, of a long-repenting murderer never quite pardoned, of an unprecedented rush to sainthood and church stardom that took Joan of Arc nearly a half millennium to achieve. And, of course, the always taboo subject of sex is introduced, but denigrated, in the customary custom—it is cast in the background, nearly as an aside.

In the case of Maria Goretti and Alessandro Serenelli, we encounter both saint and sinner and this great surge in human nature that does ensnare a man and a woman as they converge upon their joint existence.

Maria was not quite 12 years of age that hot July afternoon in 1902 when she was working in the fields. Her fellow-worker, a short distance away, could not keep his eyes off her youthful beauty.

The virile, muscular young man was enamored, hopelessly lusting for this prepuberty girl whose sensual and lovely presence haunted his thoughts and dreams and longing. The scenario presented a dream and obsession as old as mankind itself.

The grand moment of lust, linked to disaster, occurred unintentionally when the young girl's skirt stole over her legs and knees for only brief seconds, exposing the fleshy milk-white thighs to the already excited and ogling field hand nearby. Engrossed in her work, Maria never realized the brief display that spelled her doom.

From that fateful moment, Alessandro was firmly determined to claim the young girl at all cost. A would-be rapist had been molded beneath a hot Italian sky and the church would gain a saint who died protecting her virginity.

The superlatives later released by the Italian press abound. Maria had died resisting her obsessed attacker; she had died rather than submit, proclaiming to her defiler that submission would be a sin. She was a martyr, an angelic figure, an exited angel, a virgin devoted to purity of the flesh. Hers was the gift of wisdom, intelligence, purity, a saintly child's devotion that preferred death to disgrace and dishonor. In less than half a century (in 1950) she would be canonized, a saint who had died in this same century only half spent. The road to sainthood, by Vatican standards, had been traveled with the speed of light.

Now approaches an analysis that only a philosopher would dare explore. The sinner, in my eyes, must be considered a main player in the drama, no less important than the chief participant and the victim herself. For perhaps, just perhaps, without Alessandro, Maria could have died an old and insignificant person indifferent to Catholic doctrine.

No one is to really know for sure, but this analysis digs deep into the abyss of the unknown. For without the sinner, the saint, as we know her today, might not exist!

Vatican scholars will argue, and with just cause as my words are examined, and I tend to agree with the proposition, that Maria would have remained chaste and virtuous throughout her life. She would have probably died a virgin betrothed to piety. Most likely, she would have entered religious life and became a nun. Her death and martyrdom well indicated this likelihood.

I strongly concur with this theory, but, again, the philosopher pries even deeper. Would Maria, just as likely have fallen by the wayside? Without an Alessandro, to become an ordinary Italian wife and mother living out her years under more normal and expected circumstances. No one knows, but the question now sharply focuses on the "murderer," Alessandro, who eventually spent nearly three decades in prison in order to repay society and the church, for his evil deed perpetrated in the pursuit of lust on a hot and humid afternoon so many years before.

Cold, coarse, indifferent and unrepentant for many years following the tragedy, he'd emerge from his prison cell to finally transform into a sincerely contrite person asking for forgiveness. He'd live in monasteries, among priests and monks, atoning for his sin, regretting the deed that had brought him shame and infamy. He'd attend confession, receive holy communion, pray to God for forgiveness. And, Maria, herself, had lived long enough to forgive him.

Her killer would live out his latter years inundated in the Catholic faith, and die, reportedly, a virgin. The would-be rapist would die never having known a woman. His crime had assured him of his own virginity!

At Maria's canonization in Rome in 1950, the recording movie cameras would preserve for all to see, the most contradictory of scenes. For a church that preaches the forgiveness of Christ for all sinners and all mankind, I found Alessandro Serenelli strangely ignored and shunned, even misplaced. There stood the haughty and egocentric Pope Pius XII in all his regalia as he sat on his throne and pronounced the ancient Latin words that declared Maria a saint of the church and a martyr to purity.

The zoomer lens would periodically steal into the rear of the huge crowd to capture the sad image of a stooped old man standing alone and abandoned. Alessandro, still alive and ever repenting. And, apparently, never "completely" forgiven by the priests and church dedicated to the forgiveness of sins granted by the absolution of the confessional and promised by Christ Himself.

Pamphlets and books distributed and sold to the public, printed by the Catholic press, praised the new saint and her humble origins, all but ignoring the surviving and repenting Serenelli. His name mentioned alongside his horrible crime. No mention or hint of the murderer's remorse and penance. Still, without the killer there would be no victim, and Maria could have emerged less than a

saint—no one is to say. But, directly more than otherwise, Serenelli must be considered a tool of fate or an instrument of God, much in the same vein as Maria herself.

It's hard to specify exactly where Serenelli could have been properly placed and seated that afternoon in 1950, when Maria Goretti was raised to sainthood; the table of honor did not belong to him. Yet somehow, the shadow of shame deserved to be stripped from his aged and burdened shoulders that had finally been strapped by guilt, the man seeking forgiveness. If only for a few hours, he did not deserve to be cast aside and ignored in the back of a crowd. He too, was a tool of God, in a moment of frenzy transformed into an instrument molded by the youthful lust for sex, an instrument that would give the world a saint.

Without Alessandro, without the killer, there would be no Maria as we know her today—the saint would not exist without the sinner. In the final analysis, the sin emerges as of great importance as the martyr herself, for the hand that killed was also the hand that exalted.

CHAPTER SEVEN
THE BEAUTY OF CRUELTY

I was watching a popular TV talk show once that featured, as main guest, a most outspoken atheist. What I'd feel free to call an ardent God-hater, for the simple reason that I have never witnessed a man so keenly and vehemently detesting something that he claimed did not exist. In the identical breath that he denied the existence of God, he spouted his hatred for same.

It was as if he feared the very existence of the word, God. That the mere noun should not have been allowed entry into the dictionary. That a person should not have dared, or have the simple right, to pronounce the very term. If he could have had his way, it seemed the terminology would have been banished from the language itself.

As aforementioned, his stark denial simply placed him on the defensive. Why would a man so strongly and vigorously attack something that he insisted did not exist? His actual rage injected doubt in his denial.

Then, with an abruptness married to surprise (to me, the viewer), he uttered the sentence that was to remain engraved in my memory. He fairly shouted at his interviewer, his eyes mirroring his agonizing torments, his lips curled into a nasty snarl: "If a God really existed, He wouldn't have created such a horrible way for life to survive. I mean, animal eating animal; the big fish eating the smaller fish; a cat tearing a rat apart; a rattlesnake swallowing a mouse while still alive. The bloodshed and torture and cruelty that we see around us is horrible! No loving, caring, perfect God would have created this torture and misery. God is a farce!" he concluded.

The words were food for thought if only because our food chain, indeed is one studded with this obvious cruelty of one species designed to prey on another, the harsh reality of predator and prey, and the hunt is glaringly ghastly. Yet there exists a precise balance to it all, a purpose that is absolute and preordained and therefore, beautiful. In the complex design lies a rule, a law, that governs fairness as well as necessity.

It is at this sensitive juncture that the outraged atheist's words echo in my mind, and it is here that I attempt to refute his contention.

Every living thing is somehow synchronized into a clock designed for optimal performance, the second, minute, hour hands all working in harmony. No movement seems wasted or useless, our life on Earth depending on these perfected movements embedded in this delicate and precise clockwork. As for the cruelty involved, it incorporates a method that the Maker decided upon after long and wise deliberation. Every creature was designed to serve its definite purpose and attain its ultimate goal and fate. A world forever feeding upon itself must forever replenish its food supply, each generation must reproduce itself; continuation must be assured; an exact balance must prevail. And much of this assurance lies in the bloodletting and cruelty that abounds around us at every turn.

In answering that enraged atheist on the TV screen, shouting the irony of a just God creating life to be torn of limb and substance by lurking predators, I myself become a creator of sorts, at least on paper, of what I call the Eternally Useless Man (EUM). This is an allegorically inspired essay that I hope helps explain the cruelty as an accepted, even desired, necessity.

I see a man being born at age twenty-eight, what may be considered the zenith of physical and mental strength. This man is the perfect specimen, utterly handsome, virile, intelligent, absolutely likable and lovable. He is to remain at age twenty-eight and his overall physical peak, for a thousand years! Death is so distant that it can be ignored and even denied.

Not only this, the EUM is royalty, a king living in a luxurious palace. A Taj Mahal, where he commands a retinue of a thousand servants faithfully and eagerly waiting on him and his whims. Beautiful women and concubines of all shades and shapes are at his beck and call.

This guy is the supreme hedonist that can never get enough pleasure. More and more are the keywords that govern his existence. This existence engulfs decades and even centuries (remember that he'll live at this youthful, fun-filled juncture for ten centuries). But, gradually, the uselessness of his life grows like a cancer around his living carcass. He's free of all diseases but remains subject to boredom. He was born to give NOTHING back, to make no contribution, to fulfill no useful task, his sole purpose being the luxury of enjoying himself. Nothing else matters.

Of the thousands of women that he'll experience and claim, none will ever become pregnant. Food of his preference is brought to him in never-ending flows, but he plants nothing and grows nothing personally. He simply pampers himself to the fullest.

The EUM, after a mere century or two of existence, a noncontributor on a grand scale, would become bored at the emptiness in his life despite his apparent carefree lifestyle. He has nothing to give and a taker's outstretched arm becomes burdensome with the passage of time. Even his devoted army of servants and admirers, after a time, freshly replenished after each generation, has lost its respect for him and his stagnant life. The always youthful and barren women cannot express physical love for him. He is only interested in his own satisfaction and has become a bore even unto himself.

Love, one of mankind's most exclusive and elusive properties, as everything else of consequence, is alien and distant to him. For this graceful force demands giving and he is merely a taker. Love, as purpose itself, is absent.

I can't visualize the Eternally Useless Man surviving such a "perfect" existence for much more than a century or two at the very best. He'd become despondent, disillusioned, dissatisfied, and definitely suicidal. After lingering in an hedonistic paradise, served hand and foot for so long, he'd simply blow his brains out and conclude his aimless, useless, pointless adventure.

The main theme of this analysis is the lack of purpose to a life, any life, for it must possess at least the promise of a destiny, no matter how simple and ethereal. In this segment I have uncovered a rebuke to that angry atheist on the TV screen.

A mosquito is devoured by a bat; a lion ambushes a zebra and cruelly slaughters its prey for food; an alligator steals upon an unsuspecting boa constrictor and snaps it in two halves to become its next meal. And on and on in this unceasing, uncompromising saga of cruelty that studs our pulsating world. But every death has a purpose, every death serves life, every death is preordained in the makeup of a creation that feeds upon itself in order to progress and prosper. Continuity must be served.

Like the EUM, what good would it have been for this mosquito, or zebra, or boa constrictor to have lived a thousand years without fulfilling its purpose and existence, without offering its contribution.

The Creator, in His great wisdom that escapes our grasp, knew exactly what He was constructing. Violence is a vital part of our lives and the pulsating planets, stars, whirling meteors, and the constant tumult in the universe attest to same and strangely enough, a strange mixture of beauty and cruelty completes the unnerving portrait.

This touch of beauty lies in this studied statement that nothing is wasted in the economy of nature, as the EUM would be wasted. And we leave behind the enraged atheist on the TV screen wasting his time and energy hating a God that he claims does not exist.

CHAPTER EIGHT
HUMANITY'S CRAVEN ABATTOIR

The following anti-abortion article appeared in the Attleboro Sun Article, a prize-winning daily newspaper in the 25,000-circulation category, on Wednesday, October 28, 1987.

The subject of abortion is such a timely, crucial and controversial one that the author considers its entry of vital importance—the unabashed and wholesale slaughter of millions of fetuses demands exposure as well as condemnation. It's comparable to the voices of the condemned masses erupting with a deafening cry for help.

A TALE OF TWO JESSIES...
(In Midland, Texas, 18-month-old Jessica McLure was entrapped and rescued from a narrow shaft into which she had slipped. For several days, a worldwide audience watched with admiration as her rescuers toiled against the odds.)

It's a heartwarming story that reoccurs every decade or so, a tragedy that defies a tragic end, despair that despises desperation. The intensive human interest element involved offers newspapers a field day; the radio and TV media reap in their massive share of the action.

The eyes of the world focus on the startling occurrence and for a few hours and days that it endures, the peoples of the world share a common, if fleeting, embrace as their attention and imagination are harnessed together. We suddenly discover, really rediscover, that we need each other. That we share common interests and goals, that our border are as flimsy as they are artificial. People need people; the language barriers evaporate and the colors of our skin blend into one.

All of this happens because we are made to realize, in a cataclysmic event that engulfs us, that a single life is precious, that our planet is a tiny sphere, that we share and care for each other despite the politics and prejudices that abound about us. For a few hours and days, love triumphs and the peoples of the world savor real peace in the midst of a rare undertaking and adventure that has transformed into a joint venture.

BABY JESSIE ONE, a very young infant, has fallen down a narrow shaft and is entombed in a well. Unless many people of varied skills move rapidly in unison, Baby Jessie One will not survive her ordeal and the earth's bosom will encase her corpse. The television cameras dominate the scene and countless eyes watch breathlessly as dedicated men and women work frantically against time in order to save this frail little life that the whole universe has temporarily adopted as its own.

Of all the persons embroiled in the fervor of a massive rescue operation and mission, diggers, drillers, contractors, paramedics, among a talented pool of human resources, the head doctor assigned to the task stands in the forefront. He is the most visible aspect in the entire scenario. Baby Jessie One's mother depends on him most of all. The watching world believes in him and his ability as well. The ultimate result seems to hinge on this medical persona that stands at the ready the entire stretch of the unfolding drama.

This doctor, it seems, represents the deciding factor; he is omniscient. The baby must be saved. It must live. And the medical man's presence is reassuring.

BABY JESSIE TWO is also entrapped in a well and narrow shaft—in her mother's womb. And the struggling, throbbing, pulsating unborn being faced certain death, a preplanned and perfected medical technique called abortion.

The TV cameras don't glare. Indeed, the world's eyes have turned blind on the unfolding legal-medical drama. Love and care are as distant as the furthermost planet. A mother's womb, a baby's safest haven, has been transformed into a dungeon of death! There will be no heroic rescue effort, no caring worldwide audience to sympathize and observe and pray.

Here, too, a doctor works feverishly—not to save but to destroy. The baby must NOT survive, it MUST die!

After some fifty-eight hours, Baby Jessie One is pulled safely out of the earth's deadly grip. Shouts of jubilation echo throughout the world. Felicitations are in order. Not a dry eye escapes the moving moment. Joy. Hope. Love. The watching world shares a grand moment of unification and accomplishment. Of peace. A precious human life has been salvaged.

A tearful young mother hugs and kisses the chief doctor at the scene who represents the small army of workers and specialists that helped saved the child. A grateful mom is deliriously happy and the entire world participates in her moment of glory.

"I was glad to help," the modest doctor smiles. Baby Jessie One is alive and well and observers cheer.

Elsewhere, after an hour of hectic and frantic involvement, Baby Jessie

Two's doctor has concluded his work. It wasn't easy—the spunky baby-in-the-womb had been bigger and stronger than expected. In a moment of horror, a young assisting nurse had watched the strong-armed medic actually choke the tiny newborn into lifelessness. Finally, the sorry chore was over.

Save for the young nurse who had been horrified by the strangling episode, not a dry eye was evident. Felicitations are in order and a couple of aides openly applaud the doctor's unexpectedly long and dedicated complex endeavor.

An exhausted and grateful mother, her role willingly abrogated, hugs and kisses her physician. "I was glad to help," the arrogant doctor smiles.

Baby Jessie Two is dead. The world is silent. And the "humanitarians" of our age are left to rediscover their own identity.

CHAPTER NINE
PRIESTHOOD WITH A PURPOSE

It's appropriate to pay homage to a few men who were indeed honest and faithful and utterly believing in their calling and career as men of the cloth. These men are to be admired and regarded as true heroes; they are the finest representatives of a special breed that religious life attracts.

To mind comes several favorite personages who refused to be influenced by fame and fortune and who shunned egotistical pretension; they remained chaste and true to their vows.

POPE JOHN XXIII, with a paunch and a prayer

John was a "dumpy" little Italian elected pope in 1958 and who laughed at being called dumpy and worse. His reign was intended to be that of an interim pope, being 73 years of age at his election. His short reign of five years proved surprisingly useful and meaningful as he called together an ecumenical council, Vatican Two, that was to change the course of a church mired in old ways and ceremonies and bring it into more modern currents.

Above all, he was instrumental in bringing Protestant sects, and other faiths, such as the Greek Orthodox, the Muslims and Jews, in closer harmony with the Roman Church. He poured a "bit of water" in the Catholic wine of superiority and somewhat diminished typical Catholic arrogance that had permeated the Vatican attitude. His common touch and jovial warmth inspired great popular affection and appeal.

John was utterly unaffected by his rank, although he was dead serious and dedicated in his mission as head spokesman of Catholic doctrine.

A fat, physically unappealing-looking man, he was fully aware of his homeliness that contradicted his holiness. Once, shown a photo of himself and anything-but-handsome appearance, he playfully bellowed: "Gads! God knows the future and He knew when I was born that I'd become pope. Why couldn't He have made me just a bit handsomer?"

He was proven to be a wonderful "accident." His unpretentiousness was a godsend in a church studded with far too much pomp. He brought people of various denominations and backgrounds closer together, a neat achievement and a special gift to mankind. Something that the Catholic world can be proud of and appreciate.

CARDINAL CUSHING, priest of the common man.

Another towering figure in the church hierarchy who was not especially handsome and stunningly honest to the point of blunt abruptness, was this late archbishop of Boston.

As a teenager from Irish South Boston, he had worked the city subway system where his job had been to call passengers into their cars before impending departures. In so doing, those early days of shouting matches had permanently strained and maimed his vocal cords. For the rest of his life, his voice would be strained and raspy, a grating echo, much as that of a boxer whose Adam's apple had been ruptured by a solid punch. "Sound like a drunk coming out of the nearest barroom," he once remarked unceremoniously. And unceremony was his hallmark.

As a younger priest, his ambition had been to become a missionary in Central America; well into his career, he kept pestering his superiors to be assigned to this task, but he was always denied the opportunity. He was too well-known and too well-liked in his New England backyard. People trusted him and freely donated money to his charitable appeals and causes, trusting that the money would be fully funneled to its intended goal.

"When I die," he once announced when he was a cardinal, "don't look for any money under my pillow. I have no saving or checking account, no stocks, no bonds. Nothing!" And he didn't.

He was a cardinal, a prince of the church who walked around in frayed cuffs and stained frock. Once, it was reported, a wealthy Boston Jewish merchant, childless and a widower, lay dying. He called upon the cardinal to visit his bedside so that he could personally hand him his check that he felt and knew beyond doubt would be fully donated to charity if the cardinal, himself, handled the matter.

Such was Cushing's reputation. The Catholic cardinal prayed at the Jew's deathbed. The check was rumored to be close to a million dollars.

Cushing was once summoned to Rome, along with other bishops, for an official gathering. After several days in the Vatican, doing little of consequence, he exploded: "I've got important things to do in Boston. I'm wasting my time over here."

Only Cushing could be so brusque and open. It's doubtful that red-faced ecclesiastical executives of the Vatican ever reprimanded him or tried to "correct" his ways.

Another time, back in Boston, having once again been refused his request to serve as missionary in the Latin countries, his rebuttal was quickly picked up by the region's newspapers. "I collect too much money for 'em (the church)," he fairly snarled. "They'll never let me go."

Such honesty is rare in any field of endeavor. And Cushing was a rare and dedicated priest who loved and served his church to the best of his ability in his own fashion. No one could ever accuse him of hoarding or loving money. He was unpretentious in a world shackled with far too many pretensions. In the truest sense, an iconoclast in a world studded with too many icons.

A further startling example of Cushing's contempt for ceremonies and his scorn for pretension, the time-honored practice of kneeling and kissing a bishop's ring especially galled him although he never went so far as to eliminate the tradition. "A needless, outdated practice," he once echoed, sending chills up the spines of a pompous aide or two.

I would doubt that his superiors in the Vatican ever considered chastising him, publicly or privately. He was too real and down-to-earth, truly a simple Irish priest doing his best.

He was respected by Christian and non-Christian alike, a simple man of the cloth despite his high stature. He was left to his own designs, a coarse, effective, devout man walking.

FULTON J. SHEEN, archbishop, evangelist, TV personality.

A Catholic prelate who was a celebrity in his own time. Sheen was the renowned "Uncle Fultie" during the advent of television when the wide screen first captivated millions of viewers during the early 1950s. Like Cushing, he was famous and revered by Catholics and non-Catholics alike. His following and army of admirers was vast.

Unlike Cushing, Sheen's demeanor was polished and exacting. His physical appearance was more exciting and becoming. He was educated and spoke French fluently perhaps along with other languages. He was considered a neat dresser, a bit too proud and vain, and had once laughed at his attempt to appear as just an "average and ordinary" cleric. His frocks and suits were custom-tailored; no frayed sleeves and soiled sutane a la Cushing. No mustard stains on his shirt.

"I try to give the impression of indifference in my choice of clothes," he once admitted. "As if I really didn't care. I try to excuse my sharp sartorial taste by stating that a spokesman for Christ must dress the part. But really, I suppose, I'm just a bit too proud for my own good. I suffer from the sin of vanity."

Early television's first big star was comedian Milton Berle, Sheen's counterpart known as Uncle Miltie. But no matter how gifted and talented Berle's performances proved to be, the bishop with burning eyes and colorful verbal delivery consistently bettered him in the polls that measured viewers participation.

"The best actor in America," Berle once quipped. "He can name his price." In fact, Sheen was to donate to charity over ten millions dollars earned from his broadcasts and books.

So powerful and awaited were Sheen's televised sermons that numerous Manhattan cab drivers, a competitive and not-easily-moved lot if one ever existed, would halt their taxicabs to enter barrooms and other establishments; in order to view and listen to the moving Catholic evangelist who could entertain as well as inspire. Sacrificing fares and money, many of these "hacks" were Jewish or Protestant or simply non-believers.

Once, in a plush big-city restaurant while being toasted and dined by a group of laymen, probably Knights of Columbus in New York City, the celebrated bishop was "caught" pleasantly ogling an attractive and shapely young waitress serving their table. Sheen noticed, with some amusement more than embarrassment, the shocked expression on the face of one of his friends who had captured the well-known figure, vowed to celibacy and chastity, so openly enjoying a feminine landscape.

"When a man's on a permanent diet," Sheen explained, disarming his critic, "one can still look at the menu." The episode ended harmlessly on this note and failed to hurt or haunt the bishop's sterling reputation.

Sheen was a classy opposite to Cardinal Cushing, but both men, in sharply contrasting styles, despised hypocrisy. Both men believed in the worthwhile mission of their church and the "mystery" and importance of their vocation. Pope John and many other unknown clerics fit this same proud mold.

The Catholic Church has been fortunate to have produced so many dedicated servants over the many centuries of its existence.

CHAPTER TEN
GUADALUPE

I now approach the first of three episodes dealing with an apparition and manifestation that I feel can't help but impress even the hardened nonbeliever, the anti-Catholic, the staunch scoffer, the devoted skeptic and the ever-present devil's advocate.

The event must have withstood the test of time. Should an ardent doubter elect to undertake a thorough research and scrutiny in the matter, the end-result, I feel, would be fascinating as well as convincing and moving. It would leave the investigator with a glowing afterthought of the unknown and mysterious.

The initial apparition occurred at dawn on Saturday, December 9 in 1531 atop a hillock called Tepeyac in central Mexico. Juan Diego (or Dieguito) was enroute to the Franciscan mission of Tlateloloc.

The Indian foot-traveler was later to relate that he heard strains of sweet music that he associated with the flock of unnamed rare birds. The nearby mountains, he further stated, seemed to echo with their own melodic responses.

Suddenly appearing before the simple, illiterate native peon was a "lady" described as exquisitely beautiful, robed in garments which, like the moon, reflected the glorious shining of the sun. The "lady," the observer reported, requested that a temple be built in her honor, on the exact spot, promising that she would be protectress of both land and population.

Several times, Juan was to visit the bishop's residence in Mexico City. At first being coldly received and dismissed, but finally gaining admission to the cleric's inner sanctum. His tale was heard with scorn and incredibility, until at last, the Indian opened wide his tilma and revealed, in colorful tones, an engraved image of a "lady" some six by three feet in diameter.

Upon examination, expert painters and artists would later declare that the coarse material was not only unprepared but unsuited for execution. No less baffling was the apparent use of different coloring mediums; parts done in oil, or in water colors, in "distemper," while other sections displayed tints like those of flowers in bloom.

Juan also handed the startled bishop a handful of fragrant Castilian fresh roses covered with dewdrops, despite the fact that it was in the midst of wintertime December. Not only were plants frozen, but Juan's hillock was adorned with rough thistles, prickly pears, and mesquite. Beautiful fresh roses were definitely out of season and out of reach.

The tilma on which the portrait was inscribed was composed of coarse material that is easily analyzed and classified by modern standards. With the passage of the decades and centuries, Juan's garment and the images it projects has resisted all forms of decay. It survives to this very day for doubting eyes to examine and marvel at. Rough material of the identical texture decomposes and disintegrates within a period of predictable years and decades. The preservation of the original image is scientifically inexplicable.

That the "canvas" has survived intact for over four and a half centuries attests to the "strangeness" and merited devotion and awe that many have attached to the long-ago incident hurled at an Indian's feet. It places the rare and verifiable event in an exclusive class that distinguishes the European apparitions of Lourdes and Fatima.

CHAPTER ELEVEN
STE. BERNADETTE SOUBIROUS (1843-1879)

The story of Bernadette of Lourdes is a prime example of a poor unlettered girl who was "chosen" by God, or whatever celestial powers that act under godly command. She was to carry a message and warning to a mankind too unwary, unbelieving, or indifferent of its shortcomings and the wrath of the creative power that peers down in anger from "above."

The apparitions at the grotto in Lourdes were to become a leading hallmark of the Catholic world and to many "outsiders" as well. For the private events experienced by this young girl with the large expressive eyes were destined to affect even doubters who frowned upon Catholic "events."

This young, humble, unschooled peasant was to severely challenge skeptic in and out of the embrace of the Roman Catholic Church. Indeed, as is always the case where church fathers must forever guard against fraudulent claims and charlatans, the Vatican was slow in accepting Lourdes and its future saint as authentic.

In the early developing stages of the enigma at Lourdes, the word of the strange girl and apparitions spreading to the nearby villages and beyond, the throngs swelling, half a century later, a "miracle" was paramount. People wanted proof, assurance, a visible sign from "above."

Much like the shimmering, dancing sun that was to dazzle tens of thousands of witnesses at Fatima in Portugal more than half a century later. A "miracle" was mandated to occur at the scene before scores of nonbelievers. The place was Massabielle, the year was 1858, and the simple girl was to gain fame that she neither desired nor understood.

Bernadette was instructed to dig a spring out of the dry, dusty land, a command from her "lady" that sent the nervous young teenager digging in the dry, unpromising earth before some 5000 spectators that saw no miracle or sudden bubbling spring sprouting from the barren soil.

Many jeered at the agitated girl who scooped up blades of grass and swallowed them. She even attempted to "wash" herself with the dirt she had disturbed, for her "lady" had instructed her to wash from the water from the spring. In the process, to most of the throng watching, she looked ridiculous, even retarded.

The very next day, fewer than a hundred onlookers were to witness the first flow of the miraculous spring. The faithful would later come in droves to immerse themselves in the soft current; immediate cures would ensue and be recorded. The miraculous spring survives to this day.

Later, Bernadette went into a trance at one of her apparitions. Her trance bordered on an entire loss of consciousness and watchful eyes reported the following in written records: holding her black rosary in her left hand and a burning taper in her right one. The rosary hanging limply between her outstretched fingers, the flames from the thick candle began to lick the exposed fingers of the opposite hand.

A doctor named Dozous, a municipal physician with a flair for scientific study, took out his watch to time the flames flashing out at the bare fingers of the girl's left hand. Dozous was aware of earlier studies that indicated that no state of trance could resist the agony and damage of fire. The flames quivered between the fragile fingers but licked them again and again, bound to destroy at least part of the cellular tissue of the epidermis and to cause observable burns. Anyone's finger brought within measurable distance of a flame recoils almost by reflex reaction.

But the doctor saw ten full minutes pass on the dial of his watch while the flames played upon Bernadette's painless and unharmed hand. The girl finally emerged from her trance to rise and approach the niche in the grotto, as though nothing had happened.

Soon after this "vision" had come to an end, the physician examined her hand very carefully—except for a tinge of soot, it was perfectly normal.

Meanwhile, the theologians in Rome and this region of France from which Bernadette arose, were faced with an age-old problem; the girl was very undemanding and possessed no outward ambition of any kind. Her sole desire, it was clear, was to return to the anonymous circle from whence she came and live out her years as anyone else of her humble origin.

The resident bishop was to convene a commission to pass judgment on the veracity or lack of same, attached to this simple creature from Lourdes and her strange "visions." In the end, the consensus was that the peasant child was neither an impostor nor a madwoman. She indeed had been visited by the Most Blessed Virgin who had called herself the Immaculate Conception.

The girl had been touched and blessed and plagued, by a special grace. She was therefore that rarest of mortal beings destined to be honored on future altars. And a saint-in-the-making simply couldn't be let loose in an uncompromising world as some sort of ordinary citizen, subject to the deceit of an imperfect humanity. Therefore, the bishop concluded with a finality courted by sanctity, the Church of Rome had to take Bernadette under its wing and ensure permanent guardianship. She had to be planted, like a precious tulip, in one of the finest gardens, among the Carmalites or Carthusians, where the rules are strict. This would guarantee the visionary's lasting protection and preservation from outside forces ever hostile to those few touched by special grace.

Eventually, the girl, not yet fifteen at the time the above ecclesiastical observations and determination were made, would choose of her own volition, to enter a convent and become a nun. Her health would eventually deteriorate, legs and shoulders to be severely afflicted by acute tuberculosis. As she never questioned her role as the lady's "chosen one." Bernadette would never question the physical pain that would become her fate. It all represented, to her, part of a continuing message, a chore and obligation, a duty, that had been ordained from above.

A very special aspect of Bernadette's life lies in the posthumous, which proffers unshakable evidence that doubters and anti-Catholics cannot easily discard or discredit. Even the writer of this book, exhibiting many of the traits of a "Doubting Thomas" when it comes to some of the official declarations emanating from Rome from time to time, the infusion of "holy" propaganda considered a possibility, must confess his awe and admiration at the facts that have been recorded and proven. Some of which are reproduced.

The last two years of Bernadette's life were tragic, plagued by severe pain, disease lashing out unmercifully at her frail frame. Her body becoming a mere shadow, bone tissue in legs and shoulders deteriorating at a rapid pace.

Four days after her death, her corpse, despite the destructiveness of disease, did not show the slightest trace of corruption nor any foul odor. Astounded witnesses reported seeing the roots of her fingernails with the dainty pink of child-like quality.

Thirty-nine years later, the Catholic Court of Canonization appointed a commission in Nevers, which opened the sarcophagus, exhuming and examining the body in the company of several physicians. The remains, showed no sign of corruption, were nearly unchanged. The face, hands, and arms were white, with the flesh soft as though she had died only days before rather than some four decades earlier.

Her mouth was slightly opened, as though breathing, so that the shimmer of teeth was visible. The body itself was rigid and firm. The ladies of Nevers were able to lift and deposit it unharmed into a new coffin, as they would have placed a newly-dead.

The reports of such incredible and unbelievable happenings raised many voices of protest and ridicule in the alien press of an outside world, many declaring the story a hoax. The tale of uncorrupted remains was a fraud, it was stated. An embalmer of extraordinary skill, some forty years before, employed at Bernadette's death, had succeeded in some mysterious way in preserving the remains. Now a mummy was being shown off as a body miraculously preserved by "heavenly" intercession.

Seven years later, in 1929, a second commission was appointed to re-examine the remains. The grave was once again opened and the still-unchanged body exposed to a stiff scrutiny. Witnesses, onlookers, doctors and skeptics alike had now embossed the final seal of authenticity in the case of Bernadette Soubirous. The suspicions and accusations of fraud were now forever arrested. The devil's advocates were now defeated.

Lourdes has escaped the scepter of fraud. The apparitions render "living" proof that humanity rubs shoulders with the supernatural. They are unsettling reminders that there exists beyond our realm and borders and comprehension, beyond our nether world, another world beyond our reach. The apparitions also confirm that the Catholic Church, in some mysterious way, has been selected as a special conveyor to carry a very special message to a mankind famished for evidence that will encourage and support, its act of faith in the great unseen.

CHAPTER TWELVE
STE. ANNE: A PERSONAL MIRACLE

I now approach and come to the linchpin and plot. The main and sole reason and purpose why this work was undertaken. It all involves a moving personal experience that occurred in the summer of 1936, at the age of seven and a half. Which has been alluded to on preceding pages.

As I write these words, a span of nearly seven decades has sped before my eyes, but the pronounced expanse of time has failed to blur my memory or remembrance in any way. The wonder of it all has never diminished despite the passage of time. This "miracle" and the striking double manifestations just described, rank as the lasting foundation of my faith. A private, personal, bedrock faith unaffected by other various outside forces.

It is hoped that the reader will be moved by my sincerity for it would be a useless pursuit if truth is diluted by fiction or make-believe.

In those years of the thirties when the Great Depression reigned in America, the Theberge family of Lewiston knew the many insecurities and uncertainties that afflicted the lower-class French Canadian textile millworkers inhabiting that section of Maine. My mother was sickly and unemployed, but took good care of her brood, numbering four children.

We never knew hunger, our stomachs were always filled and the clothes on our backs were always clean. Yet young as we were, we sensed the despair that haunted our non-English speaking father, then employed by the Bates Mill complex that would be his place of employment for over three decades. A sixty-hour work week for the princely sum of eleven dollars!

In those early days, even large employers like Bates Fabrics did not offer medical coverage for its workers through insurance plans; such lofty innovations lay in the future. So doctors' visits and the prospect of hospitalization struck deep fear in a common millworker's breast.

In the summer of that year, I think it was the latter part of June, I entered St. Mary Hospital to have my appendix removed. This was a medical procedure bordering on a ritual. Most children, it seemed, were destined for a similar fate. Arrangements had been made. I suspect some charity was involved as the family could have been described as penniless and my stay in the hospital as an inpatient had to be of brief duration due to the absence of money—an overnight patient scheduled to be returned home in my uncle's old jalopy that served as ambulance.

We lived no more than a mile from the hospital. My uncle drove slowly and carefully in order not to harm the young patient's belly still sore and scarred from the surgeon's scalpel. I was cautiously helped to my upstairs bedroom and tucked into place. I was to remain quiet and bedridden until I fully recovered. Released prematurely I'd slowly heal and regain my strength.

It was a warm, sunny afternoon and I lay restless in my bed and prison cell. I had been operated on perhaps forty-eight hours before and I felt fine, with orders to stay put and not to exert myself in any way lest I disrupt the raw wound inside the pit of my stomach.

The window to the right of my bed was opened and stood a foot or two above a garage top. Outside, a large group of children and teenagers could be heard shouting and frolicking, as they engaged in a spirited game of baseball and other playful endeavors. I stood there, leaning on the windowsill, wanting to join the activities. I knew very well that my mother, talking to a friend on the front porch, would never allow such a move.

I quietly pulled the small, clean cardboard box from under my bed that contained my clothes from the hospital. I dressed, stole a look outside my door to make sure my mother was too occupied to observe my venture.

I carefully climbed onto the roof of the garage and immediately faced a major obstacle: how to get to the ground without the use of a ladder. I guess that something like a ten-foot drop was involved and I gave scant thought to my recent operation and my stomach's delicate condition.

I cautiously worked myself off the roof, hanging there. For a few seconds, the length of my body somewhat reduced the distance to the ground. But a sizable drop was still involved before striking pay dirt. Oblivious to the danger involved. I finally released my grip and plummeted solidly to the solid ground.

Instantly I felt the excruciating pain gripping the inside of my sensitive belly—not until this exact moment had I been so aware of the fresh scar that now decorated my belly some four inches to the right of my navel. My probing fingers were stained with bits of fluid oozing out, the sensation of the wetness repulsive to the touch.

I laid on the ground for long minutes, my body folded in agony, afraid to move lest I aggravate matters. I was entirely alone in my plight; no one was around to help me. I realized on the spot, without doubt, that I had severely injured myself. With the unfurling of this ball of intense pain, I had unknowingly begun my march towards what was to become my miracle.

    I must have lain on the ground close to a half-hour without daring to move to any extent, curled in what I would later learn to be my womb position, legs curled tightly upward with clasped hands held firmly between my knees. The spirited baseball game in the near distance, the roar of the crowd, were forgotten occurrences. I kept hoping that someone, hopefully an adult, might come upon the scene and offer some sort of help. No one was to materialize.
    The pain within my abdomen, the tearing that had just happened, was profound and agonizing. The wound was real, serious and somehow, even in these opening moments that introduced physical impairment, I feared and recognized a lasting legacy that spelled pain and misery.
    The damage was permanent and a certainty. That moment that I had dropped from atop a garage to the ground, the fall wrenching the innards of my belly, was a sad event that would hurt and harm for a lifetime. The fearful premonition was valid.
    Finally I managed to emerge from my protective shell. Inch by inch, slowly and tediously, I regained my footing, standing there with ooze-stained hands cupping my aching abdomen. It was long minutes later that I sneaked up the back stairs and reached my room without my mother's suspicions being aroused. She was still on the front porch chatting with a friend.
    I undressed, folded my clothes neatly, returning them to their box-suitcase beneath the bed. Then I crawled under the cover, weak and exhausted, eyes moist with tears and fairly fainted into sleep, unable to ignore this newfound agony.
    I told no one about my "accident," but my parents did not have to be verbally informed that "something" was wrong. I never complained, my wound had stopped dripping, but my mother, rich with a woman's intuitions, perhaps began to silently think and fear that I had had a relapse. Perhaps the doctor had botched his routine job. Perhaps I simply had been a bad prospect for even a standard operation and had failed to properly recuperate and heal.
    There were lots of perhaps involved, a lot left unsaid and a lot known despite my steady silence. Mainly, in those moneyless Depression days, the prospect of added medical services had to raise havoc with this family of a low wage-earning textile worker. Suffice to say that the scenario was

uncomfortable to all concerned and much more so to this fearing young boy whose formerly rapid walk had slowed to a cautious dragging gait.

All of this, the operation, the "accident," the aching stomach and fear of lasting misery, coincided with the planned "voo-yage" to St. Eugéne in Québec. An annual ritual and pilgrimage to Canada that defied explanation, namely, how could a poor Canadian immigrant, newly supplanted in Maine, afford to gather enough money to undertake this much-awaited return to his ancestral roots? Especially during the disastrous years of the Depression? Yet the family managed it, the "voo-yage" undertaken almost every year, the five hundred mile trip round trip a beloved ritual.

Here, my uncle, a carpenter and builder and a somewhat more successful money-earner than my father, became the dominant factor. He owned a car, what we called the Black Beetle (most likely an early Henry Ford Model T) that was as durable and dependable as it was rickety. This was same uncle and vehicle that had served as driver and ambulance to and from the hospital.

So the much-awaited trip to Quebec was again in the works and good times would overlap the bad.

For a week or so before our departure northward, the pangs of hunger and the difficulty in swallowing harassed me more and more. This was the immediate period following my stay at the hospital and my plunge from the garage top. I'd sit at the dinner table for the better part of an hour attempting to alleviate my hunger, but it proved a hopeless task. I'd hold a spoonful of food in my mouth for what seemed endless periods, chewing and re-chewing. Then, slowly and delicately I'd finally dare to swallow bit of food.

It was at this moment that the excruciating pain would grip me, as a strong-fisted man twisting at my innards. Traveling through the esophagus to its final abdominal destination, a usually normal and easy journey for a morsel of food, proved to be a fearful, painful, exasperating exercise. Downing a mouthful of food had been transformed into a major undertaking and near impossibility. Consuming a meal in part only was beyond reach.

I'd swallow as much of a bite of food as I dared at one time, the entire trajectory proving a paralyzing enterprise. The inside of my stomach seemed endowed with newly created tentacles whose sole purpose was to wrap themselves around the incoming food intake and wrack pain and torture. The inside of my stomach contracted in painful unison; a wall of resistance had been erected against the acceptance of nutrition.

Even if I sat at the dinner table for nearly a full hour, I'd fail to ingest more than a few mouthfuls; additional attempts at this forced feeding became a grueling chore. Meals became fearsome daily routines. I'd flee to the privacy of my room and silently weep. It was all a procession leading to lingering malnutrition. Even after the passage of nearly seven decades I can still recapture this hellish portrait of a young boy sitting down to confront the ordeal of a meal.

For the week or two involved, I doubt that I managed to consume the equivalency of two full-course meals. The misery endured without a lapse and I despaired, even for the relatively few days involved. But the days stretched into a week and more, my weight loss had to be as apparent as my desperation. My parents, especially my observant mother, must have discussed my plight and the sad situation in the solitude of their bedroom. Very soon, something definite had to be done or I'd wither away from the result of malnutrition; ominous indications prevailed. But it was still early and this exhibition of forced fasting was still a new experience. For the moment, panic could be delayed. But, for how long?

It was here that the annual trip to Québec intervened. For now, the urgency and shortcomings of the moment could be brushed aside—a temporary reprieve had been granted.

In those early days of the mid-1930s, for French Canadians and Franco Americans alike, the ties to the Catholic Church were solid. A visit to Quebec often meant a stopover at the shrine of Ste. Anne de Beaupre on the shores of the St. Lawrence some twenty-five miles east of Québec City and some twenty-five miles west of St. Eugéne on the opposite side.

It was here, in the bowels of the huge cathedral, that I found myself, accompanied by my mother, that humid summer afternoon of 1936. We knelt in a pew near the front of the church, my mom to the right of me.

The many altars, the countless statues and images, the mountain of glasses, hearing aids, and crutches left by "cured" believers, surrounded me. Typically, even then at an early age, I failed to be unduly moved by icons and the trappings of ecclesiastical authority. The stark display of physical-aid items discarded as the result of purported cures and miracles, to me, remained in the sphere of unknown territory, no more than a public relation gimmick designed to impress the masses.

The altars themselves, as well as the adorning statues and images, left me equally unimpressed. Yet all of this detachment for materialistic ostentation did not diminish my earnest faith in God and the power attributed to prayer. I believed in God, in the special mission of the Catholic Church. I even believed in miracles. The wonders of life and creation, surrounding us on all sides, were the miraculous icons that governed my thinking.

Even at this early stage, I somehow recognized an air of pretension, of make-believe, of propaganda, of politics and public relations, of advertising, in many of the existing schemes. I couldn't spell it out at the time, but I was already exhibiting my personal brand of independence and free-thinking. Traits that were to become integral parts of my life.

Had it not been for the miracle that had been prepared for me that very afternoon, perhaps a future of feeble faith, even a certain brand of watered-down agnosticism, could have awaited me.

But at this moment I was only seven and a half, a devout maturing Catholic whose parents, even then, wanted him to become a priest. For my part, I believed that the Catholic Church was indeed God's "only" true church. I believed in prayer and miracles and I was slowly starving to death, suffering from a ruptured stomach. I somehow surely realized that would linger throughout my life, that was promising to be of short duration.

I was afraid. I was sick and I wanted to be cured and lead a normal life.

We were both kneeling, my mother and I, engulfed in our silent individual prayers. In those days, French was practically my only language, English just beginning to make inroads. The words emerging in my mind, contrary to my lips, were slow, clear, deliberate, resounding clearly in loud echoes within my head. I prayed for a long minute, at the most, and I don't recall my exact words save for the closing sentence. I was engaged in self-styled imploring rather than with standard renditions such as the Hail Mary.

But it was this last sentence, just a few words uttered in slow mental solemnity, that became forever engraved onto my memory bank. The short seconds involved were and remain, the most startling and enduring ten seconds of my life, destined to be stored where they originated, which is, of course, the private compound of my mind. The quiet soliloquy was enunciated "inside" my head, pronounced distinctly in the French patois of my youth, but in French or English amounting to a mere nine words.

Ten seconds, nine words, and a lifetime of remembrance. As I place these sentences on paper, the decades (going on seven), numerically threaten to match and overtake the few seconds and words attached to this saga that would forever enlighten the moment and wondrous occurrence.

For the entire span my mom, kneeling to my right, remained completely unaware of the mental and physical stress and turmoil that engulfed my being.

My makeshift prayer, leading to the climactic event, was somewhat expansive, seemingly of long duration despite the actual brevity involved. But, hitting my stride and the end approaching, the forming sentence slowed to a crawl. I knew these last nine words would be the conclusion. The end of the day and the end of hope as I wished it existed. If it existed at all.

For all my youth and innocence, I did not really expect anything spectacular (or unspectacular) to occur. I would simply close my inner whispered supplication as I had begun, which was a complete lack of wishful expectation. I was as sincere as I was realistic.

My brief lamentation was intense, never abandoning this ray of childish exuberance that only a child of seven and a half is capable of mustering. The grand moment was unspoiled, void of pretension or false hope. I was merely a young lad seeking communication with a world, a force, a being that laid outside his reach but not beyond his dreams.

The final sentence etched itself indelibly in my mind, each syllable and word emerging more clearly inside my head than actual words could have ever verbally rolled off my tongue.

"Don't let me suffer the rest of my life." That last entry, LIFE, I knew to be my final echo. As it resounded inside my head and threatened to evaporate into the usual path of normal memory, a sudden and painful knot, deep inside my belly, seized my stomach. As a powerful man of great strength, his fist encased in a steel glove, mercilessly twisting and tormenting the delicate membrane that had known pain, fear and hunger for some ten days or more, ever since I had loosened my grip atop that garage back in Maine, plunging to the ground. This same stomach exposed to a lasting agony.

I bolted to stiff upright attention, my back ramrod straight, the accelerating pain intense and unbearable. With my eyes mirroring fright, I prepared to wheel to my right and hurl myself onto my unsuspecting mom's lap, seeking her motherly consolation.

But, as suddenly as it had all begun and entirely without warning, the pain snapped and evaporated! And I knew at that exact moment that I had been "touched" by some force and power that defied definition. Understanding what had occurred was beyond my grasp, as it forever remains. But it was all too real, to this very day and beyond.

I had been cured! From whatever source, from whatever power, I had been touched by this intangible thing called a miracle. And my grand moment was destined to be a private and solitary one. A unique glimpse at inner glory, a sweeping glance at the supernatural. A rare moment when the physical is aided by an unseen hand from "above." A wonderful moment of enlightenment wrapped in the shadows, but a moment that I have forever remembered with reverence abetted by awe.

But here, only seconds after it had occurred, what was I to do? I had just wanted to grasp my mother's arm or waist, to beg her relief from the agonizing pain that had throttled my insides. Now I yearned to encircle her waist and in tears, declare my exhilaration at the wondrous cure that had just freed me from a life of agony and from an early death brought on by forced malnutrition.

But would she believe me? And this thought kept at bay my open expression of wonderment and celebration that embraced me at this exact moment. For all of her Catholicity, my mother was not easily moved or convinced in matters of religion and the supernatural, despite a superstitious nature. She believed in miracles as much as I did, in the uniqueness and importance of the Catholic Church. She had to realize that I had been very sick (and would consequently see that I would no longer be afflicted). But I sensed that she'd remain dubious more than religious.

As I had never verbally expressed my discomfort or the source of my "accident" that had seen me drop from atop a garage, I feared her disbelief of the whole golden moment. So the miracle in Ste. Anne Cathedral was destined to be a private occasion. An experience relating more to the soul than to the body, something delegated to the unseen and unspoken.

Later, when I did gladly recount the event, it met with a quiet indifference from my mother's viewpoint. I doubt if she really believed me. But she did know that I had left Maine a rather sickly and shaky boy, but had returned a happy, healthy lad.

As for my father, when finally told of the extraordinary tale, I think he wanted me to believe more than believe it himself. Like my mom, he seemed unmoved and incredulous. As an old-line French Catholic, he did see a prime purpose in the entire matter, something to be salvaged, which was, of course to "give" a son to the church (a priest). Therefore ensuring his entrance into heaven. For in the old French tradition he lived by, a father who "donated" a son to the church had succeeded in gaining his place of honor in the hereafter.

"You should become a priest!" my dad more than once reminded me. "You were cured and you owe it to God!" With this admonition, he hoped to instill a sense of obligation in me and gain his priest.

I was to disappoint my father (and myself). Although I was to entertain the idea for the better part of a quarter century, until the night that I turned twenty-five while stationed with the Air Force in Germany. At that precise moment

I abandoned all thought of a priestly vocation and I must admit that I'll never be certain that I did not indeed turn my back on a calling that was carved out for me. For my miracle was real and will forever remain real.

But God, in His infinite wisdom, I feel, will allow for my lack of vision and my shallow courage in this decision that chose a mundane pursuit. I probably could have blasted off to my heavenly destination and reward with the speed of light; instead I chose a slow boat to China, so to speak.

As I have always insisted that God created us all to choose freely, then this humble human process must be honored by the creative forces. Of God's infinite attributes, His patience must be among the greatest. That our world and humanity survive as well as prosper is proof, I think of this statement's validity.

.

BOOK TWO

CHAPTER THIRTEEN
EARLY ECHOES FROM JERUSALEM

Even a Catholic who is a renegade cannot escape his Judeo-Christian, if only because Christ was a Jew and perhaps a rabbi as well. At first glance, it seems like "pious arrogance" to dare to compare myself to the very disciples who followed Christ in those distant days in Palestine. Those that saw the birth of a religion that now scans the globe. But it remains that the disciples themselves, were at first simple fishermen and laborers of the common world, before they encountered their messiah and mission.

Peter and Paul, as well as others of the original band, had to harbor doubts much like my own. They had to commit many of my identical sins. They followed, oftentimes to fall behind. Thus is isn't so strange, after all, to feel that I can rub shoulders with them as I analyze my beliefs which, I must believe, were their own in the truest sense.

The last twenty centuries scatter in the dust as I glance back to the Holy Land at the time of Jesus' birth and death. My eyes resting upon a tiny dissident sect of Galilean Jews, a frustrated and uncertain lot if one ever existed following their leader's crucifixion. They were a decapitated group seemed destined to be quickly heaped upon a forgotten slot of history.

The New Testament perhaps states it best: the broken faith of Jesus' disciples was restored when confronted by their fallen leader AND/OR the Holy Spirit who came to them during the Jewish festival of Pentecost. The meek became bold, preaching in the streets of Jerusalem.

Here, faith in the unknown pre-emptive explanation, but I feel comfortable in stating that "something" definitely overpowering appeared to have launched the disciples on a journey of martyrdom culminating with Christendom. The whole movement quite obviously, is tedious and piecemeal, a very slow process. It was hardly an overnight sensation that, as a young boy and student, I was prone to believe. It is even doubtful that the term "Christ" was used at such an early stage, say, during the first century following Golgotha.

The move toward a Christ-Lord touched a chord in many, but it also created turmoil within established Judaism. After a few decades, the movement began to take hold in commercial and cultural centers of the

Greco-Roman world. What had begun as a grassroots movement of Jewish peasants was somehow destined to become a major institution and a dominant factor in Western culture.

Today, at the very offset of the third millennium, believers and skeptics alike wonder if Christianity has lost some of the single-mindedness and clarity of vision, of the early believers.

To me, after much study and reflection on the subject, it seems that the early Christians did not see themselves as founders of a new religion. They saw themselves rather, as reformers of their Judaism. They wanted to rejuvenate, but not abandon, Judaism. But reformation in any time is difficult and the Christian message was disorganized and muddled, hardly uniform and organized. As it trudged along, it changed in many ways, especially in its depiction of Jesus, as Christianity spread from Palestine into the bowels of the Roman Empire.

Structure of discipline and authority, though appearing early on, were vaguely defined. The claims to authority were not universally embraced. Some mystical beliefs, such as Gnosticism, later condemned as heresy, may have emerged out of legitimate ways early Christians experienced the new faith.

It appears beyond historical dispute that there were real and profound differences in how the founding Christians viewed their faith. These many differences survive to our modern day as we confront the ornate majesty of St. Peter Basilica in Rome and the simplicity of a storefront tabernacle in Hispanic San Antonio, in Texas. Also from the glaring show business antics of the television evangelists to the more humble charity work of a Mother Teresa in Calcutta.

It is at this point, having made a preliminary indent into biblical origins, that I dare rub shoulders with Peter, who my church claims as first pope and the beloved "favorite" of Christ. He, whom installed him leader of the apostles and prime mover of His emerging faith and religion.

Peter, to me and surprisingly so, as I was led to believe as a youth that he was headstrong and erratic, emerges as a voice of moderation. Not only this, but Peter the great leader, is actually classified as a subordinate of James.

James, "the brother of the Lord," saw Christianity not as a new religion but as a fulfillment of Judaism. He remained a devout Jew who prayed daily in the temple and who defended the Laws of Moses until his martyrdom in Jerusalem in A.D. 62 at the hands of the Sadducees.

Discovering, rather accepting as a distinct possibility, that James, one of the twelve original disciples, was probably a Jew to the end of his life, stunned my senses! James in no real sense felt the birth of a new religion. His (and many others') belief in Jesus as the risen Messiah made sense to him only in the context of Judaism.

This development of my historical knowledge and education of the apostles and my analysis of James in particular, sent shock waves throughout my mind. Not only had James died a devout Jew, but he also had died in a manner that could be described secondary to Christianity. The shock was that I had previously been under the impression that James (as well as all the other disciples) had been a "Catholic" (long before the church had been established and the word coined).

But, be as it may, James was a leading contributor to the writings that would comprise the New Testament. His deep faith and understanding of this teacher called Christ, a real influence in what he accomplished.

In my mind-wandering into the past, I now come to the first martyr in A.D. 36. Stephen, a leader of a Hellenist synagogue in Jerusalem, he was called the Freedman. A gifted, spirited and eloquent speaker, he dared preach in the temple itself that Jewish laws had outlived their usefulness. Charged with blasphemy, he was brutally stoned to death, not because he was a follower of Christ but because he rejected the laws and rituals of his Jewish past.

My studies of early Christianity and its leading advocates astound me on two important grounds. It was far too early to call them Catholics and they often died at the hands of their own kind rather than falling martyr to "heathens." Intolerance and the eternal cry of "heresy" existed even two millennia ago and has survived the passage of the centuries to reach our shores and era.

Philip the evangelist, is the next distant figure to cross my path. Often confused with Philip the Apostle. One of the twelve disciples of Jesus, he was a leader of the Greek-speaking Christians in Jerusalem called Hellenists. His work helped hasten Christianity's transition from sect to religion.

After Stephen's death, mounting persecution struck Jerusalem and Philip the Evangelist went to Samaria where he preached abundantly. According to Acts 8:7, he performed healings and exorcisms. One of his early converts was Simon Magus, a purported "worker of magic" whom tradition links with the offset of Christian Gnosticism and what was condemned as a second-century heresy. This particular creed bellowed that Jesus was a spirit and was not crucified in the flesh.

Some modern scholars argue that the verdict of heresy, concerning this sect, may be too harsh. Gnostic writing discovered in 1945 at Nag Hammadi in Egypt, suggests that Gnosticism may have grown up alongside what became mainstream Christianity. It may even claim equal status with authentic Christian belief.

CHAPTER FOURTEEN
PROCEEDING TO ANTIOCH

Any man researching his background in order to satisfy his mind's curiosity in explaining his religion and his special brand of faith, must reach beyond the present. It is a journey that stresses the importance and grandeur of the soul, without grasping its structure or location. If the American Indian believed that even a lowly flower or a rock, as well as a blade of grass possessed a soul of its own, then I can appreciate that a human's own soul exists on a far grander scale.

Reserving a reverence for place and purpose, it is here that I reach back to the first Christians and the founding fathers of Christianity. Major locales and oases are of concern in my historical digging, such as Jerusalem and Bethlehem. As well as this place called Antioch, a strategic commercial and military crossroad in what is now modern-day Turkey. It was here that Christianity quickly took root and where most scholars agree existed a major influence on early Christian doctrine. Here is where occurred the faith's shift from a rural to an urban movement.

Most of Jesus' ministry had taken place in the small villages and in the countryside. His stories and parables are sprinkled with rural imagery. But within a mere decade of the crucifixion, the Greco-Roman city would supplant the Palestinian village as the dominant cultural backdrop of the rising religion.

It all presented momentous results; the cities became important bases for Christian missionary activity, rivaling and eventually outshining Jerusalem. The first large-scale evangelization of gentiles probably occurred in Antioch. It was here where the term "Christian" was coined, Christ deriving from the Greek word for Messiah.

According to scholars, the first Christians in Antioch probably were Hellenistic Jews who had been in Jerusalem for Pentecost, or converts who went there to preach the Gospel after Stephen's death. Many of the inspired listeners referred to the Gospel-preaching community as "Christ's people," or Christaniot. As the religion spread outward, the name stuck.

Among the first persons that structured Christianity at the offset, was Barnabas, who was dispatched by the leaders of Jerusalem who had heard of the growing Christian community and the mass conversion of gentiles. Barnabas, a Cypriot by birth and probably an Hellenist, was supposed to keep an eye on things and report back to his bosses. Instead, he himself became a leader of the community. Rather than checking the converts' activities, he led the Antiochene Christians in what became an even more vigorous movement.

Then we have the tireless missionary and theologian called Paul. A rabbi and Roman citizen and the most influential figure, apart from Jesus Himself, who initially harshly persecuted Christians in Palestine until his own dramatic conversion. Legend has it that he was thrown from his horse, temporarily blinded, and heard the famous heavenly cry Quo Vadis?

In any event, modern-day eyes scanning back two millennia must be somewhat convinced that something very special and unusual happened to drive so many on their quest to spread the word and Gospel of Christianity.

As for Paul, he established churches throughout the Roman Empire. His letters to those churches make up nearly half of the twenty-seven books of the New Testament. His teachings hailed Jesus as the "Son of God," highlighting the centrality of the cross and salvation by faith not deeds, which sharply contrasts the ancient Catholic doctrine that "good works" are necessary in order to obtain salvation.

(The German Augustinian monk, Martin Luther, some fifteen centuries later, would adopt this identical concept. Incredibly, wholly unexpected, and without warning, as these very words are being logged on paper by computer technology, in the summer of the fourth year of the third millennium (the year 2003), the pope and the Vatican have submitted and acceded to Luther's teaching and concept. The concept that faith, and faith alone, governs man's alliance with his God, being the sole wherewithal assuring salvation. And so it has been since the advent of the new millennium and the year 2000.

In effect, for the very first time in its long, turbulent and obstinate history, the Church of Rome has now publicly and officially bowed to an "outsider's" dictate. This very same principle mirror's the author's own view, being the driving force that spells his independence. Faith, and faith alone, even without any knowledge of Luther or the Vatican, is the gift, the power, the force, and the obsession that controls, and has always controlled, my life.

Returning to Paul, he traveled an estimated 10,000 miles throughout the Mediterranean region in his journeys. His eloquent argument against the authority of Mosaic laws, at the Council of Jerusalem in A.D. 45, assured Christianity's growth from a Jewish sect into what was to become a worldwide religion. He and Peter would be martyred in Rome.

By the end of Emperor Nero's reign, in A.D. 68, all of the apostles would be gone.

That Christianity changed dramatically in that first generation or two is beyond question. What is subject to debate is whether those changes reflected inventiveness of the first Christian missionaries or the "organic" development of what WAS already present.

In their struggle to understand what it meant to accept Jesus as Messiah, the early Christians left no easy answers. Some two thousand years later, there's much cause to ponder.

CHAPTER FIFTEEN
FACING CHRIST AS AN EQUAL

To even dare to confront an ideology that has survived the test of time and attempt to place it on an even keel with this writer's and researcher's mind and ordinariness, is a task that is both formidable and audacious. In Christ we have a persona that has flowed down to us from the writings of bygone, mostly nameless scholars who were also ordinary in similar ways. But who was exactly, this lone man who roamed the desert and outlying villages preaching the "word of God?" Was He, too, ordinary in many ways?

It's interesting to note that even in the twentieth century such a devoted and sincere Christian physician and missionary to Africa, Albert Schweitzer, concluded that the historical Jesus could NOT be proven. Schweitzer accepted Christ strictly on the basis of faith, as must be the case for all Christendom.

Still, approaching the subject of Christ on an equal footing, considering Him a fellow human being in the context of it all, presents both a dilemma and a challenge of enormous proportions. Knocking Him off His pedestal, if only temporarily for analytical purposes, is more sacrilegious than audacious. But church teaching and doctrine have always proclaimed that Jesus was indeed a man first, the offspring of a woman, albeit it a virgin sired by a strange and wondrous force called the Holy Spirit.

Yet all followers must remain somewhat comfortable with the knowledge that Christ, during His brief sojourn on Earth, had to wear sandals and mix with other men of His time and place; thus exchanging thoughts and seeking revelations that we all seek. If Christ was born of woman and died a human death, as is documented, then one must be allowed the luxury of confronting Him as a man and an equal.

It is only through men's eyes that other men can be measured and assessed. So the study begins as we enroll the help of others. And there is one striking contemporary of Jesus who influenced Jesus Himself. The lone and sole figure in historical text who can be described as a teacher to the teacher.

John the Baptist (8-4 B.C. TO c. 27)

According to all four Gospels, the precursor of Christ Himself. Born in

Judea, son of priest Zacharias and Elizabeth, cousin of Mary, the mother of Jesus.

John was a Nazarite from birth and prepared for his mission by years of self-discipline in the desert. About age thirty, he wandered in the region of the Jordan Rive, preaching penance to prepare for the imminent coming of the Messiah. He baptized penitents with water as symbol of the baptism of the Holy Spirit that was to come. With his baptism of Jesus, his role as precursor was accomplished and his ministry came to an end soon afterwards.

John angered Herod Antipus, Judean ruler, by denouncing him for marrying Herodias, wife of his half-brother Herod, and was imprisoned (see Luke 3:1-20). Upon the request of Salome, the beautiful daughter of Herodias and Herod, John was beheaded (see Matthew 14:3-11).

In art, John the Baptist is represented wearing a garment made of hair and often carries a staff and a scroll bearing the words Ecce Agnus Dei (Behold the Lamb of God) (ref. John 1:29). In the West, his birth is recorded as June 24, and his death as August 29.

John the Baptist is the only figure in biblical history to have been allowed to actually overshadow Christ if only for a fleeting moment. Even today at the advent of the third millennium the Baptist is revered by a small and unique religious group called Mandeans in present-day Iraq. This sect regard Jesus as an apostate.

With the Baptist, a daring comparison has been made, placing, if only for a moment, Christ on an equal with a contemporary. In so doing, the Baptist represents humanity as a whole confronting his maker. For a single second, mankind stands on an equal footing with the godly.

It is a stunning surprise even to educated people in historical data, to discover that even today in the advent of the third millennium, that the little-known sect of Sabaean Mandeans exists in Iraq, where they gather annually on the banks of the Tigris River for their Golden Day of Baptism. Their religion dates back from sometime in the first three centuries A.D., perhaps earlier.

Its tenets and practices reflect a mixture of religious influences: ancient Gnostic, Jewish and Christian. Somehow they reflect an exodus of early followers from Palestine to Mesopotamia. Mandean leaders estimate that some 10,000 of their followers remain in Iraq, with various small groups in other countries around the world. They are neither Jewish nor Muslim nor Christian, but their faith bears similarities to each. They claim their own sacred book, the Ginza Raba, which includes the book of Genesis. They believe Adam to be their first messenger. They also regard Christ as a false messiah. Their creed proclaims John the Baptist as the most important teacher.

When they pray, Mandeans face north, using the North Star to orient themselves; in this fashion they believe they are facing God and the forces of light.

CHAPTER SIXTEEN
CHRIST REVISITED

Some modern scientists now theorize that homo sapiens evolved, not merely from a lowly beast or animal such as a monkey or gorilla, but from a mere earthworm that crawled over the Earth millions of years ago. A step further (or lower) is the report that researchers in a California cave have discovered a super microbe that eats iron and thrives in the equivalent of battery acid. This microbe, reported in the *Journal of Science*, was a previously unknown organism. Some scientists further speculate that such a microbe superseded the earthworm, or dolphin, or monkey, or whatever other evolutionary rungs exist leading to this being called homo sapiens.

What we have is the first unambiguous evidence that is able to bridge the anatomical gap between lower and higher primates. The Creator's handiwork is never diminished in the process.

Be as it may, the wonders of creation cannot be overlooked or downgraded by whatever final determination to be rendered, in an advanced scientific age for evolution is also part of God's blueprint. Whether man emerged from a lowly microbe or bacteria, or worm or fish or animal, is unimportant. For God's purpose remains unchanged. Life on Earth survives as our most precious commodity, our most valuable gift and cherished treasure.

Also created and subject to the evolutionary process in this elusive substance called faith, the one ingredient that all living creatures MUST exhibit. Faith is the only element and prerequisite that the "heavens" insist upon. It is a cry that must be more than a murmur. It must be a crescendo heard far beyond the borders of our solitary planet circling in orbit amidst an immense sea of other planets that clutter the endless, fathomless universe.

It is the power, acceptance and ownership of faith that has led this lone human being and writer into this complex literary venture that seeks to divulge a truth hitherto concealed from view and from mankind itself. It all begins and ends with a short phrase echoing from ancient Scriptures, simple words few in numbers, their clarity and simplicity extolled: . . . and God created man in His image.

It is here that man reaches an epochal, decisive moment of self-discovery, the above seven words ringing in his ears. This is the very beginning of the Theory of Spiritual Evolution as it looms before our eyes and understanding. Claiming that the Creator is creator and that lowly man is capable of creative powers. That he can actually reverse and redesigns things in his own image, appears preposterous, until we study the last hundred years that have sped by us, with their fantastic advancements that have altered our very fate and future, our lives and thinking. We have stumbled upon an age of discovery that outstrips previous dreams and expectations. Man is now already re-creating and refining his world. And it is only the beginning of monumental achievements.

Robotics are in the offing, in their very infancy, machines designed to replace man's drudgery in the workplace are promised. Technological wonders are sprouting around us on a daily basis, changing our mode of living as well as our thinking. These changes in our physical world must definitely reflect the changes in the spiritual sphere. For our physical presence has been enhanced a thousandfold and our spiritual awareness has simultaneously undergone its own dramatic metamorphosis.

Thus God has created all things. Man eventually standing on the summit of this creation. Now man has reached the ultimate point where he'll create his own God, completing the cycle established eons ago when the master architect loosened his vast binding handiwork.

It is at this delicate, meaningful, fruitful and revealing moment that the writer-thinker scribbles these words. He is striving to unravel a mystery wrapped in a mystery, seeking to uncover an answer to a seemingly unanswerable query.

Now approaches the main study and analysis: where is, what is, this product that man has conjured and created as his own image, or God?

The first insight lies in examining this ancient tribe of Israel that was forced into exile some two thousands years ago. They returned to their historical homeland in Palestine in 1948, within the lifetime of the author of this book, and in line with predictions ascribed to ancient writings. All indications point to the Jews as having been God's preferred people or simply the first out of the starting gate. But something appears to have gone awry. The original Jewish tribe emerged from central Greece millennia before Christ, eventually to be replaced as main emissaries destined to compose their final act in this drama, where the created would create his own God.

Was John the Baptist next in line probably selected to carry out the role consequently accorded to Jesus of Nazareth? There are indications that this could have occurred, but again, as with the original Jews leaving Greece, we are left in a void. The search for a replacement continues.

The process transformed into a collective one with the rise of countless religions and cults and beliefs sprouting on every continent, generation after generation. From the faiths of the East and the Orient, from the depths of China, from prehistoric times to the present modern age with its abundance of high technology, the West somehow emerged as a predominant force destined to complete and solve the perplexing problem and puzzle.

Which brings us to the origins of Christianity and Jewish mysticism and the Dead Sea scrolls that serve as a sort of Rosetta Stone, that enlightens our investigative venture.

My Theory of Spiritual Evolution is a startling concept that crept up on me almost subconsciously, yet the seed of its future growth had to be fermenting somewhere in the depths of my mind all along.

If Darwin saw the physical world evolving from some sort of meekness and smallness transforming into strength and bigness, the fittest surviving and reigning, then why not apply this same principle to the spiritual sphere? Much more than this premise, the unseen spiritual aspect somehow outweighs that of the solid and physical presence that surrounds us. The entire study and conclusion are based solely on this intangible power called faith. A force repeatedly recalled and praised in this study. More than a mere thought, faith nearly emerges as a god.

This belief is fueled by that ancient biblical phrase: God Created Man in His Image. A handful of words accurate and meaningful beyond their brief scope. They bellow God's presence at the dawn of Creation. They actually announce His intention and plan of having man share in the creative process—before all things, all forms of life, all objects vibrant and inanimate, are to be returned to their original state of nothingness. Before oblivion beckons, the cycle completed, and the Maker has reclaimed all that he has granted.

The created had to create his own God, in his own image, in the very same fashion that the Creator Himself had launched His master plan in the very beginning.

All along, with a muted awareness, man has been engaged in this process of erecting his own god. Over time a game of celestial trial and error has been played and replayed. The true God has observed man establish his many religions, erect idols and temples to various deities, build monuments and icons that he sought to invigorate with life and meaning. Statues were prayed to as if alive and blessed by a higher power. The real God watching in disbelief as man stumbled time and again. Man's unending forays into this remote land of the invisible and supernatural seemed destined for disaster and failure.

Yet each new century saw a new breed of believers that advanced slowly and unceasingly toward their final destination, that promised unity with the unknown. Slowly and painfully mankind was emerging from its ignorance, God watching, at times on the verge of impatience and anger. Man was forever climbing to greater heights, inch by inch, aspiring for things that promised far greater rewards than life and death alone. It seemed to offer him in a curtailed life span frayed with hardship and uncertainty.

How would, how could, this flimsy creature called man ever rise from his lowly estate to create his own god? It seemed an impossibility, an unrealistic goal and task, but it remained the pivotal part of God's design, as the accelerated half-dozen or so millennia have served to illustrate.

CHAPTER SEVENTEEN
THIS SEEDLING CALLED JUDAISM

At this juncture, a background study of the original Jews is required. They appear to have been the original "chosen" people of God. The first architects to erect and duplicate the Creator's image. Why were they eventually downgraded, sidetracked, or even replaced? Why was their mission and commission derailed? Those are questions that evade an easy answer.

But the Jews were special in the scheme of things. They remain special, to this very day. The centuries of exile that they endured, the pogroms and persecutions that span the millennia, generations and countries, attest to the sufferings that have been their lot. In the twentieth century that has just passed, the world has seen Hitler's "final solution," which left millions of Jews exterminated. The exact reason for such hardship is left dangling, but a reason must exist.

Who were the Jews? All that is known is that they emerged from central Greece centuries before the era of Christ. The now-famous cache of scrolls discovered in caves at Qumran between 1947-1954, on the western shore of the Dead Sea, written in ancient Hebrew with some Aramaic and Greek words thrown in, offer a fresh, updated insight unavailable to scholars of previous times. Indeed, the scrolls arrived just in time, as a freak coincidence, for our modern eyes to examine. This accidental trove of information simultaneously takes us back to early Judaism, as well as to Christ and his apostles. The fabled Holy Land of antiquity and the inhabitants that walked its lanes, for at least a brief spell, are clearly visible.

But it was one of the scrolls, which was secretly "kidnapped" and hidden from public awareness that catches our eye. It was revealed to the world at large but a handful of years ago, and holds the key opening history's door to heretofore unknown and undreamed of data and revelations. And a glance at the earliest Jews and their inroads is also presented.

If this "lost" stone is never proven to be a fraud and I believe the test of time will confirm its validity, it represents one of the most stunning discoveries of the ages.

The stone describes a mystical, angel-guided tour of the heavens. It mentions Sons of Darkness and Sons of Light, numerous lines echoing the gospels of the New Testament. EL stands for God. Bellal for Satan.

Most incredible is an angel supposedly addressing a listener as the "Son of Man," again echoing the New Testament. Not only this, but mentioned explicitly by name is Yeshua, son of Padiyah, a term in ancient Hebrew for Jesus! As for the phrase, "Son of Man," Jesus Himself purportedly applies this line in depicting Himself.

Thus the "lost" stone, retrieved from the shore of the Dead Sea at the midpoint of the twentieth century and predating the Christian era by many centuries, serves in forging a vital link to ancient times. Also the importance of the Jews as a "chosen" people who were somehow delegated to a role of lesser impetus, while remaining key players in the long-ago drama of heaven and earth engaged in its baffling ritual of mutual creativity.

The ancient Jews are a stepping stone from the old to the new, from a Moses to a John the Baptist. To a Jesus of Nazareth to the moment that Faith-be-God held hands with God-the-Son, who now belonged with God-the-Father. It is here that this family called Trinity will find fulfillment. It is here that mankind will find its niche. At this point in archaeological history, the twenty-first century and third millennium already breached, it appears a fair assumption that the ancient scribes of Qumran, now called the ESSENES, a sect of ascetics and mystics, were an offshoot of the original Jewish tribe that emerged from the Hellenistic world. More than this, it can be argued that the Essenes were the precursors of the doctrine of a coming Messiah, who will redeem the world, in effect, the coming of a Christ the Savior.

What we observe, with a clarity that was unavailable only a half-century or so ago before the discovery of the caves and scrolls at Qumran, is man's first concrete attempt to unravel his origin and purpose for living. It is completing the cycle of the created having harnessed all of the forces and ingredients in existence and at his disposal, to re-create (uncover) his Maker.

It is here that the fulfillment of the archaic phrase rings out with majestic truth and splendor: "And God Made Man in His Own Image!" And man, all alone in his experiments, has been assigned the immense task of duplicating and completing the cosmic puzzle before him.

The third millennium just now upon us has seen the evolutionary process rise from its infancy; the physical aspect has encountered its contemporary, the spiritual.

CHAPTER EIGHTEEN
A TOUGH TASK: CHOOSING THE CHOSEN ONE

Approaching this segment represents a herculean effort, a delicate matter and a sensitive allegation, for what is entailed is a search for a reason why one member of a species or a single species as a whole, has been favored over another in bringing a "message" to the created from the Creator. Involved is the complex assumption emanating from an individual's mind (the author's) based on a lifetime of reflection, acceptance and rejection before reaching final conclusion that is always flexible and subject to change.

It involves a prolonged journey into a nebulous sphere outside of the physical. An exploration into the unknown where discoveries are unveiled. If unveiling is denied, then the explorer is forced to produce his own road map and seek a new landscape emerging before his eyes.

It has therefore been my contention that the Roman Catholic Church has been selected by the contracting forces to spread the "word" among the masses that trample over the Earth, the past, present and future cramped into a single space. As if the wonders of creation are not ample in their own right, as if the numberless stars and planets of our inexhaustible firmament are not enough proof of a handiwork requiring a masterful controlling mind and skilled captain at the helm. We have the additional aid of what can be called a bonus celestial incentive that has studded the centuries in order to further impress and convince the believers and nonbelievers alike that God not only exists but DEMANDS recognition through this substance, or tool, or vehicle, called faith.

It is here that the handful of simple words from ancient biblical text erupt before our eyes with volcanic fury, a warning as well as an admonition. "Mine is a Jealous God," is a phrase not to be ignored.

Returning to the grass roots and the question of WHY one particular source has emerged as chief "messenger" of the word. This advocate is the Catholic Church as we know it today. It presents a controversial assumption, for, at first glance, it rings with an unmistakable tone of arrogance for the recipient of the credit—but a background analysis tends to firmly support the theory, discarding this same element of arrogance from a church and religion that often basks in its presumed superiority.

Yet why has the Catholic Church, in all its weakness and strength, emerged as the "anointed" leader in this mission of celebrating and propagating this power of faith, established as the primary gift by the Creative Power from the very offset that saw its handiwork placed in motion?

Again, to this student of history engaged in composing this literary work, his personal prejudices, beliefs, and convictions huddled into the sincere inspiration that propels his pen, based on some three-quarter century of life spent on a reflective journey of the mind seeking enlightenment, sincerity abounds, although it remains but one man's viewpoint.

To the forefront again marches these columns peopled by members of the Jewish tribes, ancient and modern and even futuristic, these enduring survivors of pogroms and unimaginable slaughters—these same contributors and disciples of faith that predated the Catholic appearance upon the scene, the Jews who superseded the Christians as procurers of the message from "above."

The Jews were not necessarily replaced, but they were derailed and placed in a secondary mode, as perhaps numerous other cults and religions that have crossed and conquered the obstacles and hurdles of man's historical existence. How many others like the Jews, have been sidetracked only to be supplanted? No one knows and no one will really ever know, for the records of man's tortuous trek lie buried deep beneath the sands of time.

Now, at the very advent of the third millennium, we have the imposing presence of the Catholic Church, the ultimate messenger. This claim buttressed but such factors as the stunning manifestations at Lourdes and Fatima, not-of-this-world experiences that allot mankind added insight and encouragement in its quest to recognize and embrace this ethereal substance called faith.

With all its drawbacks and imperfections, the Catholic Church has established itself as the leading voice instilling faith into the bosom of a diverse and divided populace. Forgotten and forgiven are the church's many faults, i.e., the flimsiness of many of its ceremonies (though ceremonies are of much importance) and its reluctance to change, tradition honored for the sake of tradition alone (although tradition too plays an important role).

Also noted is the centuries-old problem of sexually abusive priests that have preyed upon young children, pedophiles that number not in the hundreds but in the thousands. The scandals mostly swept under the carpet and the offending priests reassigned to new distant parishes, and the commission of further abuse, in order to "protect" the clergy's reputation, such as is the case in the United States at this writing, the church undergoing a crisis of massive proportions.

But regardless of the many defects, the Catholic Church strongly appears to have been "chosen" to be the leading force, the main teacher preaching the power and beauty of faith to the universal masses.

Even with the premise of a Catholic supremacy, an intriguing query remains relevant: is this Christian-Catholic mission destined to endure, or like the Jewish movement before its presence, ultimately fated to be unloaded by the wayside and replaced by yet another cult and messenger? The author, for one, believes that the dye has been cast, that the Catholic Church is the final heir apparent to this thorny throne that seats both servant and slave proclaiming the "word" of God and the necessity of faith.

Only yet unwritten history holds the final answer to this query, and history as lonely man confronts and perceives it, can be a short stroll across the street or an endless flight across the eons.

CHAPTER NINETEEN
A PARTING GLANCE AT EVOLUTION

After nearly a decade of off and on composition and harnessing of thoughts and pen, commencing in the early to mid-1990s and concluding in the first few stanzas of the third millennium, the book is finally facing its closing word and chapter.

But how is it that the mental evolutionary process, which has been so forceful in my life, remained, for the most part, so submerged and stagnant in the scheme of things? For evolution, as time itself, flows abruptly, undisturbed, unstoppable in its progressive path, a cerebral function that will not be denied, even though it nearly slumbers on the sidelines and shadows of an individual's makeup and existence.

As I wrote and rewrote, evolution of the mind and spirit forging headlong in this intellectual process that surges up and down in unsuspecting ways, progress demanded slow recognition. I became enthralled by this nearly dormant giant lying forever beyond view of this obstructive mountain range that overshadows the everyman who walks, such as I, thinking and rethinking his role and place in this drama called life and death.

I eventually became more than merely stunned to discover that I dared question, even alter, age-old teachings which, in my youth and personal background, spelled ancient and embedded Roman Catholicism. In time, indeed much time, I would cast my personal heritage aside, placing it on the so-called back burner of priorities while I strove to become my own man and thinker.

Then, suddenly and overwhelmingly, seemingly without design and almost void of preplanning, I confronted creation itself. There stood before my eyes my own insignificant creation, this nurtured human being that would trek atop this planet for merely a handful of fleeting decades, this next-to-invisible dot wedged amidts billions of other dots pockmarking the world beyond.

The tools, the place, the plan, the know-how, the required skills and experience, the very essence that the scheme of things demanded, nay! Preordained, all was waiting a master carpenter's handiwork, had been languishing for its day of reckoning.

That man, particularly this man and writer of ordinary talents and low estate, would be one to embark upon such a complex journey and endeavor, proclaiming this equally ordinary and lowly species called the human race, was actually seeking and searching for the pinnacle of creation. The created, all along and alone, had had this vision and duty and calling to uncover, mold, and "create" his own world and destiny. Only in this fashion could the future exist and be explained, only in this way could life be fulfilled and embrace its purpose.

Why else would all the necessary tools be strewed around him in such abundance? Why else would man progress day by day, century by century, eon by eon, forever seeking the purpose and reason for his existence? It is in this vein that the biblical phrase, "Man Was Created in God's Image," suddenly strikes with full force in reverse fashion, for it is man who, in turn, is procreating God in his own image!

Thus it is that spiritual evolution maintained a foothold in my life and in the life of all of us. In the end, the puny transforms into the mighty—creation confronts its completion. And, in the bargain, humankind has fulfilled its primary task of having deciphered the very meaning of the creative powers that surround and engulf our lot and destiny.

In the final analysis, the created will have projected his own image into that of the Creator, the two having merged to become one.

So it is that all things will be renewed. That the perfection of creation will be fully attained, that the beauty of the universe will be honored and protected. So it is that good will have conquered evil. The might and grand purpose of eternity no longer questioned and subject to the imperfections that have plagued our lot and kind since the dawn of time. It is here that the end will spell the beginning, that the new sunrise will overcome the oppressive night, and that man will stand on an even keel with his God and Maker.

Approaching the end of this chapter and Afterword, these closing words seem to belong more in the realm of the Foreword, where the author was preparing to review anew the incidents in his life that comprised the elements that constructed the thoughts and theories that had emerged. The acquired reader who has read this far, it is hoped has embarked upon a literary venture that he found worthy of his time and effort. For the author's part, I dare proclaim that I have derived a fair measure of satisfaction and a feeling of accomplishment as my pen is all but prepared to rest. It has all proven to be that heralded labor of love that lies in waiting for every man who travels over that long and winding road of life.

CHAPTER TWENTY
STRANGE BEDFELLOWS:
THE POPE AND MARTIN LUTHER

The Summing Up

Striking the final chapter and closing lines of this deeply personal, yet basically universal, philosophical in-depth study, the writer is compelled to review that main aspect that motivated his literary venture into the nebulous sphere that every human being visits and revisits during his abbreviated life span upon this speck of a planet that is surrounded and inundated by innumerable other specks, and even galaxies. It is that stretch beyond his vision and his vision's imagination, for the might and power of the creative handiwork, numerically as well as figuratively, lies far beyond man's own ability and power of comprehension. The dizzying numbers and seemingly impenetrable space involved, buried beneath the sands of time and eons, overwhelms man's curiosity that steadily clings to his intellect.

Most surprising and unexpected, even alarming, was "The Theory of Spiritual Evolution" that seemingly inched forward in snail-like fashion from an obscure background, emerging from the backwaters of the mind and thinking process, where it had lain apparently dormant amidst its dominant presence.

In the beginning stanzas, during the off and on years of reflection and returning to the chore, spanning nearly a decade, the term "evolution" was actually limited and linked to the renowned British naturalist, Charles Darwin and his now-famous "Survival of the Fittest" analogy.

Now, abruptly, the physical connotation stripped of its veneer, the visible catering to the invisible, the unseen's eloquence rang greater than that of the seen and touchable. Almost effortlessly the puny man had dislodged his mental blinkers, transfixed by a mind-scope usurping the landscape, this frontier land of thought and learning a newly discovered wonderland, almost godlike in its capacity to lure and captivate the nearly oblivious seeker. For this unseen, but gnawing force called spirituality had cast its fleeting shadow upon the overall scene. Its presence now undeniable. The unique realm of the spirit had been broached by a short-lived, puny human being who sits upon this orbital express destined to travel but a short distance in the annals of celestial enterprise.

Thus it was that spirituality was encountered, a stepping stone to an even more startling and stunning theory and supposition, man's mind facing an even greater challenge and adventure as it dared to steal a peek into that long, bottomless pit called creation. This stolen glimpse of this astounding, complex, and sublime masterpiece attached to the mysteries of eternity itself.

If spiritual evolution crawled out from the so-called mental backwaters, where it had laid in wait nonetheless, an unintended surprise and revelation. Then the next and second surprise disclosure must also qualify as a nearly unannounced guest and element, what rates as anti-climactic—that creation itself can be diluted, dissected, reconstructed, reclaimed, and virtually be recreated by the lowly handmaidens that have evolved from its midst and energy. In this case none other that this creature called homo sapiens, resulting in the striking finale when the Creator's entire workload and gifts and magical handiwork have all been established to serve mankind. This final link in this colorful, conflicting portrait more blinding than the sun at its apex—despite his two brittle and perishable hands. Man has now selected to compose this grand epic that will strike the final chord in this grand opera where two worlds collide and become one, much as a man and wife becoming one flesh and being—man, in the end, will have duplicated the Maker's and Master's achievements.

How else can be explained the volcanic developments and advancements that have occurred at this juncture of our third millennium?

Man has escaped, and is still escaping, his enslavement to pettiness and the unimportant. It has all proven a long and trying process, a long day's labor, but the tools of a planning, constructive God surrounds our lot, to be grasped, studied, and finally utilized into a grandeur that's comparable to the overall setting imposed upon our pulsating planet.

This past half-century (the latter part of the twentieth) has seen thundering advancements in knowledge and technology, highlighted by man's landing on the moon in 1969, the laser, maser, the invention and introduction of that astounding piece of machinery called the computer, which among countless chores, can analyze millions of data in micro-seconds.

Still lying in its cradle of infancy, the computer already foretells of an adulthood of sporadic quantum leaps, but a simple tool among multiple other tools still awaiting to be unlocked, examined, and utilized.

So man now stands on the threshold that will launch him to even greater heights in this new age seeking definition and completion.

If man, at this writing, is confronting many other means of self-development, this burgeoning influx of computer technology but a sample of things to come, its overpowering presence is a stunning event. It is curious to try and imagine what similar power already exists in the celestial establishment lying beyond our own. At this point, biblical excerpts echo from the wilderness with a strange clarity and added meaning, all pointing to the Creator and created strolling hand-in-hand toward a mutual meeting ground—The Last Shall be First; The Meek Shall Inherit the Earth; The Weakest Shall Overpower the Strongest.

Therefore man hovers, prepared to stampede onto the plains of his inherited destiny. He was created in God's image and this same God, perhaps often time impatient and tormented, awaiting this closing episode that will see theory transform into fact.

Thus was born, in this writer's and philosopher's mind, this vision that meshes God and man into a single entity, creation begetting creation, beauty reflecting beauty, good overcoming evil and sin. All of this extraordinary energy expounding a third novel theory that was mainly unknown and undisturbed at the beginning of this literary endeavor: that man was chosen and selected (but never forced!) to decide, decipher, construct, rebuild, and finally redistribute this abundance that has been strewn across his path with that purpose of planned procreation foremost in the scheme of things.

So man is struggling, sacrificing, thriving, and aspiring, day by day, inch by inch, second by second, thought by troubling thought, to reach this loft goal of confronting his Creator and the very purpose of his existence.

If both spiritual evolution and the recycling of Creation nearly evolved as surprising blockbusters not distant from "accidents" as this book progressed, articulation forming the crux of the matter, a third element surfaced to share in the title of "Unsuspected Revelations or Developments." From the very offset, faith has been heralded as the primary force and catalyst that forged and encouraged the written project; but what was practically bypassed and overlooked was the inclusion of the main messenger of this doctrine that is proclaimed of such paramount importance in the scheme of things.

What was most amazing was the slow recognition of the chief architect of the "word" who was none other than the controversial German Augustinian monk Martin Luther of Elsleben.

With Luther, the writer has run the full gamut, from detestation to indifference, to acceptance to admiration. At the very beginning, the mostly obscure excommunicated priest was a dark and ominous shadow, best to be avoided and ignored.

In my early Catholic upbringing and education under the helm of capable Dominican nuns, some of them hailing from faraway France, the "old country" itself still referred to by some, if erroneously, as Catholic France, Luther's name was loathed. He was the perennial "bad priest," a Judas, an evildoer, a monk untrue to his vows and vocation if one ever drew breath.

At the start of this book, Luther was meant to be no more than a passing reference, a footnote, a necessary evil, if you will, but still worthy of mention if only because of his undeniable historical role in the Reformation.

But as the book reached its twilight stage and after nearly a half-millennium spent in the restricted isolation imposed by smallness, (Lutherism's important but limited numerical presence) Luther's full impact and his affinity to faith suddenly sprouted in full bloom.

I had always felt it a certainty that the Catholic Church would eventually join hands and forces some decades or even centuries after my passing, embracing and welcoming the many Protestant sects, but before reaching the conclusion of this book the unsuspected occurred, advancing my mental timetable with a floodgate rush.

On October 31, 1999, in Augsburg, Germany, the Roman Catholic Church and the Lutheran World Federation signed a joint accord, The Joint Declaration on the Doctrine of Justification, representing an ecumenical event of historical significance.

From the Reformation perspective, justification was the crux of all disputes. For Lutherans it retained special status, it was obtainable by faith alone. For Catholics "good works" had to accompany the belief.

The arguments were ancient as well as forceful, and both sides obstinate in their approach. The rationale: all human beings are in need of God's righteousness "since all have sinned and fall short of the glory of God." (Rom 3:23; cf. Rom 1:18-320; 11:32; Gal 3:22; "for the righteous will live by faith.")

According to Lutheran understanding, God *justified* trusting in faith alone (sola fide). Thus the faithful can rely on the mercy and promise of God, despite his own weaknesses and manifold threats to his faith, on the strength of Christ's death and resurrection.

In accord with the Second Vatican Council, the Catholic Church declared, (thus joining and embracing Lutheran thinking) to have faith is to entrust oneself totally to God who liberates us from the darkness of sin and death, awakening us to the prospect of eternal life. Thus flows the unsolicited and unmerited gift of faith, grace and justification.

A simple yet startling comparison and parallel that both confirm and strengthen this claim of this undeserved but existing gift that is faith, is our own birth, everyone's birth. That happens to be the gift of life which is granted without "payment" or "precondition" or any other "demand" of retribution for that unearned and unmerited spark of life which was implanted and loosened not because of our merit but because of the *promise* (Velkd 94, 20-24).

So it is that the Joint Declaration of 1999 in Augsburg discards any and all condemnation of the Council of Trent which was so critical of the Protestant movement. Together, Catholics and Lutherans now accept the newborn credo, by grace alone, in faith in Christ's saving work, and NOT because of any merit on our part. We are accepted by God and receive the Holy Spirit who renews our hearts...

So it is, with these unexpected and rapid developments, that Martin Luther of Eisleben has emerged as the greatest precursor of the doctrine of faith, the loudest, clearest, most stirring voice to be heard in the past thousand years of Christianity. It is splintered by rabid infighting and division by members of numerous sects devoted to a common deity. Without exaggeration and going beyond the last millennium, Luther's voice can be considered an extension of John the Baptist's own evangelism.

Rather than an avowed troublemaker and iconoclast bent on destroying the papacy in a time that it was draped by greed and excess, mired in corruption that raised widespread calls for renewal and reform, Luther has suddenly and surprisingly taken center stage as a unifying voice which, after nearly five hundred years, is only starting to be distinctly heard and appreciated beyond the compounds of the Reformation itself.

One particular Luther biographer noted that on his deathbed the defrocked Augustinian monk expired much amidst ceremonial decorum reserved for a Catholic prelate in "good standing." None other than Pope John Paul II, during the pre-Augsburg era, praised Luther's religiosity and his commitment to Christ's and the power of faith

Who is to say, in this rapidly changing religious climate, that Luther's excommunication will never be lifted? Perhaps he did die more a dedicated priest than an outcast and transgressor.

One thing is clear and certain at the beginning of this literary project; to the author, in the beginning, Luther was considered no more than a footnote darkened by deed and defeat, unworthy of much laudatory mention, if any. Now, almost without warning, and a welcome sight it represents, Luther is a beacon of enlightenment, of strength, hope, charity, all these intangible attributes which, like faith, respond to our innermost hopes and aspirations lying beyond the realm of human merit or understanding.

Printed in the United States
27757LVS00005B/295-297